Walk of Remembrance- Trilogy Pa

Walk of Remembrance

by

Richard Terrain

Walk of Remembrance- Trilogy Part 1

Walk of Remembrance- Trilogy Part 1

FADE IN:

EXT. ROUTE 476 - OUTSKIRTS OF PHILADELPHIA - NIGHT

A three-lane highway relegated to one lane. The serpentine line of cars bottlenecks as it slithers by. An arch of ORANGE AND RED FLARES outlines the area of shattered glass and twisted metal.

We are at the site of a gruesome car accident. An ambulance and four police cars are on the scene. Two cars are involved in the crash. The first, a SILVER CADILLAC with its front caved in a perfect semi-circle; there is no-one inside the car.

The second car is a different story entirely. A DARK GREEN HONDA PRELUDE crushed against the concrete median that separates the South-bound lanes from the North-bound lanes. All the windows have imploded. The original seventeen foot length of the car, compressed to ten. The hood has folded back into the front seat. This car is not empty! Through

Walk of Remembrance- Trilogy Part 1

the sliver that used to be a window, WE SEE a female hand, purple, swollen and bloody.

Some drivers have stopped their cars on the shoulder and have walked over to the flares. A set of cops wave them back.

              POLICE OFFICER
Get back in your cars and continue
  with the traffic. There is nothing
    you can do.
     (beat)
  Get back in your cars...

CUT TO:

OFFICER PIERCE speaks to a female OFFICER DANA.

              OFFICER PIERCE
  What's the story?

              OFFICER DANA
  She's been dead about ten minutes.
  The jaws are on the way... Ran a
    license check. Her name is Ellen
    Parker. Forty-two years old.

Walk of Remembrance- Trilogy Part 1

                    OFFICER PIERCE
          What about him?

Pierce gestures to a HISPANIC TEENAGER who is cuffed behind his back and being led to a police car.

                    OFFICER DANA
          D.U.I.

                    OFFICER PIERCE
          Shit... How old is he?

                    OFFICER DANA
          Seventeen. It's his grandfather's
          car. On his way back from drinking
          with the 'boys'.

Pierce lets it sink in.

                    OFFICER PIERCE
          Who do we contact for her?

Dana checks the papers in her hand.

                    OFFICER DANA
          Her husband. Maurice Parker. They
          live in Wynnewood. Married
          seventeen years.

Walk of Remembrance- Trilogy Part 1

Pierce looks back at what remains of the HONDA PRELUDE.
Beat.

                    OFFICER PIERCE
      There isn't any good left in the
      world, Dana. Not one damn thing.

CLOSE UP of the hypnotic RED AND BLUE LIGHTS that consume the highway.

DISSOLVE TO:

EXT. ROAD - EARLY MORNING

                "TWO WEEKS EARLIER"

Just AFTER DAWN. A gentle mist hangs in the air. The calm suburban streets wait to be flooded with a sea of middle class homeowners on their way to work...

A woman's REEBOK CROSS-TRAINERS move along the sidewalk... long, brisk steps, steps people have when walking with a purpose...

Walk of Remembrance- Trilogy Part 1

The Cross-Trainers enter the doors of a bakery store seconds after a man turns a window-sign from "CLOSED" to "OPEN"... This happens with precision timing, not losing a step... a well practiced routine.

CUT TO:

INT. ANGELO'S BAKERY - MORNING

ANGELO, a large man, black slicked hair -- has laid out three identical loaves of RAISIN BREAD on the counter.

     ANGELO
  Very good batch today.

We finally see the person standing in the REEBOK CROSS TRAINERS... MRS. ELLEN PARKER, a woman in her forties with a heart-warming smile and wise glint in her eyes. The kind of woman that somehow becomes more beautiful with age.

She carefully squeezes each loaf. Her hand hovers over the middle loaf.

     ELLEN
  That one.

Walk of Remembrance- Trilogy Part 1

CUT TO:

INT. KITCHEN - MORNING

Twenty minutes later. The basket of the "chosen" raisin bread is placed on the center of a table. Ellen covers it with a cloth napkin.

The eggs sizzle in a pan. We find Ellen cooking breakfast. A stunning African Grey Parrot sits proudly on Ellen's shoulder. CLAUDE is a breathtaking creature with grey feathers and a cherry red tail.

The DOOR BELL RINGS.

CUT TO:

FRONT DOOR

where a delivery man hands over a bouquet of VIOLET ORCHIDS. Claude, still perched on Ellen like a clothing accessory, spreads his impressive wings defensively. The delivery man scans the far wall to find a collection of bird photographs.

Walk of Remembrance- Trilogy Part 1

A dazzling collection of all kinds of birds, elaborately framed and hung.

Ellen signs the release and closes the door. She takes a deep smell of the violet orchids and looks down the hall to the open bedroom door with a glowing smile. We CATCH A GLIMPSE of a man dressing.

CUT TO:

KITCHEN

Where Ellen and her husband are eating breakfast. Claude is now in a cage in the hallway.

MR. MAURICE PARKER eats a buttered piece of raisin bread. He is a man in his late forties, neatly combed hair, his New York Times folded into a manageable rectangle. This is a man who has been seated a great deal of his life... the type of man who breaks into a sweat when taking out the garbage.

He feels a stare and looks up to find his wife with that glowing smile. He smiles back.

Walk of Remembrance- Trilogy Part 1

*Ellen gestures with her eyes to the violet orchids now
displayed proudly on the window ledge.*

              MAURICE
    Yes?

              ELLEN
    The flowers... they're beautiful.

Maurice studies them.

              MAURICE
    They are... who sent them?

Beat. This takes Ellen by surprise. Maurice catches the expression.

              MAURICE
    You thought I sent them?

              ELLEN
      (disappointed)
    There was no card.

Maurice reaches over and searches the bouquet.

              MAURICE
    Have I forgotten something? Is
    this a special day?

Walk of Remembrance- Trilogy Part 1

>   ELLEN
>   (flat)
>   It's just a regular day.

Maurice pulls out a small bent card from between the stems.

>   MAURICE
>   It's from Dan and Kate Wilkins...
>   for dinner last week...

Maurice hands Ellen the card, she looks at it uninterested.

>   MAURICE
>   It's a special day isn't it?

>   ELLEN
>   Well, I'm sure it's not Christmas,
>   because you'd be worried about how
>   much money we don't have to spend
>   on each other... I know it's not
>   New Years, because you'd be going
>   on and on about wearing a tuxedo
>   and how much you don't like to

Walk of Remembrance- Trilogy Part 1

              dance... and I'm sure it's not our
              anniversary, because I didn't find
              an envelope with a hundred dollars
              cash on my bureau with a note that
              says, 'Pick out something pretty'... Yes -- Maurice -- I'm
              virtually certain it's not a
              special day today.

Ellen begins to eat. Maurice stares at her...

                    MAURICE
              You're mad at me... You were
              beaming a minute ago, but since I
              didn't send the flowers... now
              you're mad at me.

Beat.

                    MAURICE
              Why would I send flowers? What's
              the occasion.

Ellen instantly becomes emotional.

Walk of Remembrance- Trilogy Part 1

                    ELLEN
          Occasion? Because you
love me...
          That's the occasion.

Ellen returns to eating. Maurice
stares at her quietly.

CUT TO:

INT. BOOKSTORE - MORNING

A SHAFT OF LIGHT penetrates the
darkness of a room... growing
LARGER as the door swings open.

Ellen steps in first followed by
Maurice. Ellen goes
straight for the blinds. BURST OF
LIGHT stab the room.

The spines of the BOOKS catch the
light... rows and rows of
books cradled by a maze of mahogany
book shelves. This is an
old-fashioned store with antique
chairs at select places. A
coffee table sits near the window
with a set of deep
cushioned sofa-chairs. This store
is a home...

Maurice moves behind the counter
and TURNS ON THE RADIO.

Walk of Remembrance- Trilogy Part 1

CHOPIN FLOWS from the old speakers atop the corner shelves -- delicately.

Ellen opens the door to the store and locks it in that position with a slanted piece of wood... The store is now open.

CUT TO:

INT. BOOKSTORE - DAY

Half a dozen people wander the isles. Maurice's eyes drift to a pair of eleven year olds who have sauntered into the store. One boy disappears behind "Philosophy" and reappears momentarily with his sweat-shirt zipped up to his neck -- a rectangle is outlined under his shirt.

          MAURICE
    I see that!

Maurice comes around the corner -- the boys HAUL ASS out of the store. They're long gone before Maurice reaches the door. He yells after them.

          MAURICE

Walk of Remembrance- Trilogy Part 1

> I'm getting a Doberman! Two!

Ellen who is sitting in the back room doing the accounts, comes out when she hears the commotion.

> ELLEN
> You've been saying that for two years; I think they know you're bluffing.

Maurice inspects the "Philosophy" section.

Maurice looks up as a young man, early twenties, hurries in. KRIS REDDY walks past Maurice, his black locks of hair peeking out from under his Philadelphia Eagles cap.

> KRIS
> (to Maurice)
> Lizy Bennett?

> ELLEN
> Hi Kris.

Kris waves as he removes his jacket. He is wearing a PARKER BOOKS T-shirt underneath. He pins an "Assistant Manager" tag

Walk of Remembrance- Trilogy Part 1

on.

Maurice thinks to himself.

                    MAURICE
    Lizy, Eliza... Elizabeth Bennett...
        (the answer comes to him)
    Pride and Prejudice.

                    KRIS
    You're amazing.

                    MAURICE
    It has to be a full character's
    name.

                    KRIS
    They called her 'Lizy' in the
    book...
        (beat)
    Sorry I was late. My jeep died on
    the way over from the paper.

                    MAURICE
    They printed your article on, 'Dry
    Verses Can Dog Food'... Very
    enlightening.

Walk of Remembrance- Trilogy Part 1

> KRIS
> Pulitzer, here I come.

Kris notices as Maurice goes back to searching the isles.

> KRIS
> What happened?

> MAURICE
> Never have children. If they're
> not a burden to you, they're a
> burden to someone else.

> ELLEN
> (on the end of his words)
> Kris, go to the pharmacy. Ask Mr.
> Donnavan to get you a large bottle
> of Geritol... Tell him, Maurice has
> officially become a grumpy old man.

> KRIS
> What'd they take this time?

> MAURICE
> Nietzsche!... As if they're going
> to read Nietzsche.

Walk of Remembrance- Trilogy Part 1

Maurice moves back behind the counter clearly irritated.

      ELLEN
  They pick on you because they can
   get a rise out of you... children
   can sense those things.

Kris quickly opens his black shoulder bag and pulls out a mini-tape recorder. He talks into it -- dead serious.

      KRIS
   Monday -- August 24... Juvenile
   delinquency -- Are the victims to
   blame?

CLICK. The tape recorder returns to the bag. Ellen stares at him curiously.

      KRIS
   Story ideas. I'll forget them
   otherwise.

Ellen nods with realization. Ellen and Kris turn their attention to Maurice who is mumbling to himself angrily. He

Walk of Remembrance- Trilogy Part 1

looks out the window to the street to see a familiar group of school boys waving at him tauntingly.

CUT TO:

INT. CHINESE RESTAURANT - NIGHT

DIMLY LIT. Red and gold paper mache lanterns are sprinkled around the room. WE FIND Ellen and Maurice polishing off a dish of General Tso's Chicken.

          MAURICE
   Two thousand square feet... We can
    add a used book section.

Ellen is not listening. She is staring at a young couple two tables over, who can't take their eyes off each other.

          MAURICE
   Next door is a jewelry store with a
    full-time security guard... He
     stands outside all day. Let's see
    them try and take Nietzsche then...

Walk of Remembrance- Trilogy Part 1

Maurice finally notices Ellen is not listening.

                MAURICE
      Ellen?

                ELLEN
        (snapping out of it)
      What?

                MAURICE
      The new store?

                ELLEN
      Honey, I told you. If it makes you
      happy, we should just do it.

                MAURICE
      It's a tremendous amount of work --
      moving.

                ELLEN
      We can do it together.

Maurice needed the support. His face brightens.

CUT TO:

LATER

Walk of Remembrance- Trilogy Part 1

An empty table. The dishes have been cleared. Maurice and Ellen are opening their fortune cookies.

                    MAURICE
    What's your's say?

Beat.

                    ELLEN
    ... Love is shown through actions
    not just words.

                    MAURICE
    What's that? That's not a
    fortune... You will be rich...
    That's a fortune. What you have is
    a statement.

                    ELLEN
    What it is -- is the truth.

                    MAURICE
    I don't follow.

Beat.

                    ELLEN
    Maurice, what would you do for me?

Walk of Remembrance- Trilogy Part 1

What would you do for our love?
I'm not talking about saying, I'm talking about doing.

Maurice notices the STRAIN IN HER VOICE.

          MAURICE
Is this going to be similar to the flower incident?

          ELLEN
      (very emotional)
Sometimes people need to see things done for them -- because sooner or later they don't believe the words anymore.

          MAURICE
      (raising his voice)
You don't think I love you?

Customers react.

          ELLEN
      (lowering the volume)
I want to be shown...
      (beat)

Walk of Remembrance- Trilogy Part 1

          Maurice would you do anything for
          me?

                  MAURICE
          Yes.

                  ELLEN
          Anything?

                  MAURICE
          What do you want from me? Would I
          swim across an ocean for you?...
          Would I walk across the United
          States for you? Yes... Yes I
          would. You know that.

                  ELLEN
            (soft)
          No I don't. I don't even know if
          you'd walk across the street for
          me.

Maurice is getting redder by the second. The entire restaurant hangs on his response...

                  MAURICE
          So what have you done for me that's

Walk of Remembrance- Trilogy Part 1

so earth-shattering?

The waiter closest to the table cringes with Maurice's words. Ellen drains of color. She stares at him in complete and utter disbelief. She drills him with this iron glare for an eternity then grabs her purse and heads to the exit. Maurice stares at the table for a moment to gather what's left of his dignity and follows her out.

The waiter moves to the table and clears the aftermath. He sees Ellen's fortune crumpled next to her tea cup. He unravels it. The fortune reads...

"YOU ARE A FRIENDLY AND GENEROUS PERSON."

CUT TO:

INT. BEDROOM - DAY

The room is LIT BY ONE BEDSIDE LAMP. Maurice is sitting in bed wearing a robe. Reading glasses at the end of his nose as he rubs a yellow cloth over a SILVER MEDALLION. The medallion has a raised picture of a lamp, the kind Aladdin uses, seated on an open book and the words BOOK SOCIETY - 1992. Maurice meticulously rubs away the smudge marks.

Ellen is at the edge of the bed -- as far from Maurice as possible. Her back is to him as she sleeps under the covers. She speaks without turning around.

> ELLEN
> Why do you polish that thing all
> the time?

> MAURICE
> You're talking to me?

> ELLEN
> Why do you polish it?

Maurice studies the impressive silver medallion.

> MAURICE
> A Book Society Award is a very
> prestigious thing.

> ELLEN
> Why are you polishing it -- in bed
> -- in your pajamas -- at 11:15 at

night? Are you going to show it to
someone?

                    MAURICE
          No.

                    ELLEN
          Then why?

                    MAURICE
          There's no reason.

                    ELLEN
          Exactly. No reason. No occasion.
          It just makes you feel good to do
          something for it, to express your
          pride and affection for it some
          how...
              (beat)
          How come you'd do that for a piece
          of metal and not for me?

Maurice has no answer. He just stares at his hands.

ELLEN'S face can be seen under the covers facing away from
Maurice. Her eyes are red. The tears roll off her nose and

land on the pillow unseen and unheard.

CUT TO:

INT. KITCHEN - MORNING

The kitchen table is mockingly empty. No bread. Not even a crumb. Maurice, dressed for work, eyes the table with great resolve. He rubs his hands together ceremoniously.

     MAURICE
  I can do this.

Maurice moves to the fridge and gets out two eggs, onions, green peppers and mushrooms.

CLAUDE is chirping INCESSANTLY FROM THE HALL.

The pile teeters precariously in Maurice's arms as he moves to the counter. Next the pans come out -- He tries to pull the bottom pan from the cabinet --

CUT TO:

BEDROOM

Walk of Remembrance- Trilogy Part 1

Ellen is seated in bed, arms crossed -- equal resolve in her face. A LARGE METALLIC CRASH OF POTS ECHOES FROM DOWNSTAIRS. Ellen grabs her robe.

CUT TO:

HALLWAY

Ellen gently takes Claude out of his cage. She kisses him. The bird, once frantic, instantly at peace.

>   ELLEN
>   (whispering)
>   You missed mommie... worried when I
>   didn't come down... my baby... so
>   sweet.

Ellen feeds the bird as she peeks around the corner, careful not to be seen. Maurice is desperately trying to cook an out of control omelette. It spills over the sides and SIZZLES on the range top. He tries to scoop it up with the pan, tilting it further -- further -- the entire omelette slides onto the range. Maurice frantically tries to wrangle it back in. Man

Walk of Remembrance- Trilogy Part 1

vs. Egg. Man losing.

Ellen has to keep herself from laughing. Her expression changes to pity as she watches the chaos unfold.

CUT TO:

INT. BAKERY - MORNING

Ellen scrutinizes a new three loaves of raisin bread.

                ELLEN
    That one.

Angelo smiles and packages the chosen loaf.

CUT TO:

INT. KITCHEN - MORNING

A defeated Maurice is eating an apple. He looks up with surprise as Ellen walks into the kitchen from the back door, a bag under her arm. She glances at him and then moves to the counter where she prepares the bread for serving. Ellen looks down into the trash to find the rebellious omelette

Walk of Remembrance- Trilogy Part 1

sitting uneaten.

The bread gets laid out in its usual basket, in its usual manner. Maurice says nothing as Ellen pulls two eggs from the fridge and cracks them on a sizzling pan with expert ease.

                    ELLEN
          Onions?

Maurice smiles warmly at his wife's back before moving to her and hugging her from behind. He whispers in her ear.

                    MAURICE
          Why do you put up with me?

Beat.

                    ELLEN
          Love... has something to do with
          it.

Maurice reaches over and turns off the stove. He then turn Ellen around and kisses her long and hard. Ellen pulls away gently and stares into his eyes. Maurice looks very emotional.

Walk of Remembrance- Trilogy Part 1

>   MAURICE
>   I do love you... very,
> very much.
>
>   ELLEN
>   Show me.
>
>   MAURICE
>   (with all his heart)
>   I will -- I promise.

Ellen kisses Maurice and returns to the eggs. Maurice continues to hug her from behind. The MORNING SUN pours into the kitchen covering Ellen and Maurice in a golden bath.

CUT TO:

INT. EMPTY STORE - AFTERNOON

A large black man wearing a dress shirt, sleeves rolled up to the elbows TURNS ON a switch. A SET OF TUBE LIGHTS FLICKER TO LIFE.

CARL STONE leads Maurice out to the main room which is presently a cob-web infested, barren space with a few discarded packing boxes left in the corners.

Walk of Remembrance- Trilogy Part 1

Maurice runs his fingertips against the wall.

                MAURICE
    History and the arts will be
       here...

His hand makes a grand swirl pointing to another area. He says the next two words with great awe as if he was saying something holy.

                MAURICE
      The Classics...

*Carl watches curiously as Maurice walks around in a trance.
He moves to the bay window that over looks the street.*

                MAURICE
    We'll have a hand-painted sign...
       (another grand swirl)
    ... Parker Books.

Maurice's already bright eyes, brighten even more as he spots the security guard strolling up and down the front of the jewelry store. The guard catches his stare and waves.

Walk of Remembrance- Trilogy Part 1

Maurice is aglow... He turns to Carl.

                  MAURICE
    This is my dream... it's finally
    here.

Carl has to smile -- rarely does he see someone so happy.

CUT TO:

INT. OFFICE ROOM - AFTERNOON

We are in Carl's cramped upstairs office... just enough room to walk amongst the file cabinets.

Maurice holds his pen over the documents before him.

                  MAURICE
    I wish my wife were here. She
    should see this...
       (stalling)
    She had a doctors appointment in
    Blue Bell. That's a one and a half
    hour drive. Ellen's been going to
    that doctor since she moved to

Walk of Remembrance- Trilogy Part 1

>>>>>>>>>>>>*Pennsylvania...*

>>>>>>>>>>CARL
>>>>>>>>>>>>(understanding)
>>>>>>>We could do this tomorrow?

>>>>>>>>>>MAURICE
>>>>>Ellen gave me strict orders to sign
>>>>>>it... We invited some friends over
>>>>>>-- you see, for a celebration.

Carl smiles patiently, he's seen this before.

Maurice gathers his strength as he puts pen to paper... He scribbles his signature quickly and let's the pen drop to the table top as if all the energy drained from his body. He looks up to Carl with powerful eyes.

>>>>>>>>>>MAURICE
>>>>>>Every journey begins with one step
>>>>>>>>right?

Beat.

>>>>>>>>>>CARL

> Enjoy your party Mr. Parker... Your
> new store will be waiting for you
> Monday morning.

Carl and Maurice shake hands like best friends.

CUT TO:

INT. HOUSE - NIGHT

A wine chiller sits proudly on the coffee table. The SOUNDS OF LIGHT CONVERSATION float through the room. About ten friends and family have gathered.

Maurice sits on the sofa nearest the window. He's listening to the drone of TED PRICE.

Ellen is not present.

>   TED
> ... So she says the "L" word, after
> two dates, the "L" word! She says
> 'Don't you believe in true love?
> Love that can conquer all?' I say,

Walk of Remembrance- Trilogy Part 1

>   *'Whoa, hold on. Just so we're*
>   *clear on things, I think love these*
>   *days is shit. It don't mean a*
>   *thing and it don't stand for*
>   *nothing. Shit.'... You know what*
>   *she says, 'Fine, but how do you*
>   *feel about kids?'*

Everyone near the SOFA LAUGHS. A CAR LIGHT DANCES ON THE CURTAINS... Maurice quickly pulls the curtain aside and watches as the car pulls past the house and around the corner. Maurice turns back from the window hiding his concern and without missing a beat...

                    MAURICE
          It's nice to see you don't have any
          scars from your divorce.

This brings on another ROUND OF LAUGHTER.

THE TELEPHONE RINGS.

Walk of Remembrance- Trilogy Part 1

*Maurice rises from his seat -- but is waved off by ADELLE
MATLIN who picks up the phone right away. Adelle is
Maurice's niece, early thirties, very attractive and always
smiling -- except at this moment.*

*Ted begins another one of his stories -- the words are
incoherent as Maurice watches Adelle carefully... Adelle
turns her back to the room as she talks and then DISAPPEARS
into the kitchen stretching the phone cord around the
doorway... Something is definitely wrong.*

*Maurice steadies his gaze at the door of the kitchen...
eternal seconds pass before Adelle appears again. She looks
different -- ghostly. She glances up for a fraction of a
second locking eyes with her uncle -- she immediately looks
away.*

*Maurice watches Adelle move to her husband GERALD and
whispers in his ear. Gerald changes instantly -- taking on
the same ghostly transformation -- his eyes dart to Maurice.*

Walk of Remembrance- Trilogy Part 1

Ted's story is cut off as Maurice speaks LOUDLY...

              MAURICE
    What's wrong?

The room goes SILENT as all eyes fall on Adelle and Gerald.

              GERALD
      (shaking)
    Maurice, can we go into the dining
        room?

Beat.

              MAURICE
    What's happened to my wife?

This hits everyone in the room like a bomb. A dread hangs over every passing second... Gerald crumbles under the moment... Adelle begins to cry.

              GERALD
    There was a car accident... Drunk
        driver.

Some of the crowd reacts. A women covers her mouth. The moment is unbearable.

Walk of Remembrance- Trilogy Part 1

                    MAURICE
                 (to himself)
            Please God -- don't do
this.

Gerald cracks -- the tears start to
flow from his eyes.

                    GERALD
            Maurice, it was
serious... I don't
            know how to --

Gerald buries his face into the
heels of his palms as if
trying to contain an explosion in
his head.

                    GERALD
            Oh Jesus, please help
me... She
            didn't... Ellen didn't
make it...
            Ellen's dead Maurice.

Maurice closes his eyes shut
tightly... like a child scared
of the dark.

Adelle blacks out, knocking over
the wine chiller on the way
to the ground. In less than a
minute the room has
transformed from a celebration to a
mourning. Everyone is

Walk of Remembrance- Trilogy Part 1

frozen staring at Maurice for their cue... A child in her mother's arms begins to cry as if aware of the circumstances.

EXTREME CLOSE UP. Maurice opens his eyes slowly. The room stays still as Maurice stares at Ellen's HAT sitting on the piano.

DISSOLVE TO:

EXT. PARKER HOUSE - MORNING

A "FTD" Florist truck pulls up. A delivery man, moves with an extravagant bouquet of flowers to the front door. He RINGS THE DOOR BELL. No answer. KNOCKS. No answer.

The delivery man looks to the ground and searches, before placing the bouquet on the porch.

WE NOW SEE that the porch is completely covered with flowers, bouquets and wreaths. The delivery man tip-toes his way through the maze of condolences and moves to his truck.

CUT TO:

INT.   KITCHEN - MORNING

Maurice waits, as the SOUND OF THE FLOWER TRUCK FADES AWAY,
then looks into Claude's cage. Claude sits on the highest
perch and continues to call to his mother. Maurice stares at
the pile of untouched food on the floor of the cage.

                    MAURICE
          Eat the food Claude...

CUT TO:

LATER

Maurice seated at the kitchen table.

He looks at the bouquet of flowers still seated on the window
sill. The violet orchids are all dead and shriveled up.

DISSOLVE TO:

INT. PARKER HOUSE - NIGHT

The house feels abandoned -- lifeless.

Walk of Remembrance- Trilogy Part 1

*THE HOUSE IS SILENT EXCEPT FOR THE
FRANTIC CHIRPING OF CLAUDE
FROM THE HALL. His hopeless cries
punctuating the air every
few seconds.*

CUT TO:

BEDROOM

*Maurice sits in a chair facing
Ellen's wardrobe closet. The
LIGHTS IN THE ROOM ARE OFF. The
room is lit only by the
LIGHT FROM THE HALLWAY STREAMING IN
AT AN ANGLE.*

*Maurice gets up and with a great
deal of uncertainty, opens
the closet. Maurice stares at the
collection of hanging
dresses.*

*He reaches out and pulls the cloth
of a floral dress towards
him... He closes his eyes and
smells the cloth... his face
tightens in pain... both hands
cling to the dress tightly...
he tries desperately, can't fight
it -- Maurice Parker begins
to cry.*

*His hands grab frantically at the
rest of the dresses --*

pressing them to his face and chest.

                 MAURICE
      Oh God... I'm sorry Ellen... I'm so
         sorry...

He hugs the dresses as if they were her. His weeping turns to a torturous wail of grief... all the love, all the anger spilling out in this one moment.

He falls to the ground yanking all the dresses down with him -- they collapse atop him... He buries his face in his wife's clothes...

The MUFFLED SOUND OF HIS CRIES ECHOES through the lonely house.

DISSOLVE TO:

EXT. PARK - MORNING

The neighborhood park. The trees in full bloom. Maurice walks down a path leading to the open fields. Only mothers with strollers and the elderly are out this early.

Walk of Remembrance- Trilogy Part 1

CUT TO:

PARK BENCH

Maurice is seated on a park bench. Across from him is an ELDERLY COUPLE -- in their seventies. The OLD WOMAN is frail with tiny eyes that disappear when she smiles. The husband is a skinny man with a baseball hat that makes him look like a little boy.

Maurice watches them silently as they sit and hold hands... Their warm laughs and whispered conversations stinging him. He watches as the old man gets up. The old woman tries to make him stay, but he playfully pulls away. She shakes her head like a shy school girl as the old man walks back down the path by himself.

The old woman glances Maurice's way.

          OLD WOMAN
  Good morning.

          MAURICE
  Good morning.

Walk of Remembrance- Trilogy Part 1

The old woman glances at the empty baby carriage standing next to the bench.

>   OLD WOMAN
>   Is it a boy or a girl?

>   MAURICE
>   Oh, that's not mine.

Maurice gestures to the woman and baby who are sitting on a blanket in the grass.

>   MAURICE
>   I don't have kids.

>   OLD WOMAN
>   You should. Children are a
>   blessing from God. I have four.

The old woman studies him.

>   OLD WOMAN
>   Are you okay?

Beat.

>   MAURICE
>   Is that your husband?

She nods, "Yes."

>   MAURICE

Walk of Remembrance- Trilogy Part 1

>   You look so happy -- how long have
>   you been married?
>
>   OLD WOMAN
>   Forty-seven years.

This hits Maurice hard.

>   OLD WOMAN
>   Are you married?

This hits Maurice even harder.

>   MAURICE
>   (this is painful)
>   Yes... Seventeen years.

The old woman looks down the path for her husband.

>   MAURICE
>   Where did he go?
>
>   OLD WOMAN
>   He's getting my sweater from the
>   car. I said there was a breeze.
>   (shaking her head)
>   I told him not to go.

Beat.

>   MAURICE

> May I ask you a question that might
> sound strange?

                        OLD WOMAN
> Yes.

Beat.

                        MAURICE
> How do you know he loves you?

The old woman looks at him oddly.

                        MAURICE
> I mean besides... time -- how did
> you know ten years ago -- twenty
> years ago?

She thinks hard... tough question. No answer for a moment then --

*The old woman sees something out of the corner of her eye --
her husband is walking up the path with her white lace
sweater over his arm...*

She smiles as the answer comes to her.

                        OLD WOMAN

Walk of Remembrance- Trilogy Part 1

> Because he shows me... he's not
> much for words, but he shows me.

Maurice sits back -- her answer lingers in the air like a haunting voice.

Maurice watches as the old man comes back and drapes his wife with the sweater. The old woman waves as they continue down the path... hand in hand.

CUT TO:

INT. DOCTORS OFFICE - DAY

An obese woman with a hacking cough sits to the left of Maurice... To the right, a man with a patch over his eye.

> NURSE
> Parker... Maurice Parker.

The nurse sticks her head outside the glass divider till Maurice stands up.

CUT TO:

EXAMINATION ROOM

Walk of Remembrance- Trilogy Part 1

DR. ROYCE checks a chart. Maurice watches him from his perch on the examination chair.

                DR. ROYCE
So what's the deal Maurice?

                MAURICE
Pardon?

                DR. ROYCE
I mean why the sudden voluntary
visit -- usually it takes gun-
point to get you in here...

                MAURICE
Routine, I assure you. I just
wanted to gage my health. Am I
healthy?

                DR. ROYCE
Yes -- you are.

                MAURICE
I'm going to ask you a question
that may sound peculiar.

Walk of Remembrance- Trilogy Part 1

Dr. Royce folds his arms and waits... What's this all about?

                    MAURICE
     How far could an individual walk if
     they had no athletic training --
     you understand, just an ordinary
     person?

Dr. Royce stares at him suspiciously.

                    DR. ROYCE
     I know what you're getting at.

                    MAURICE
     You do?

                    DR. ROYCE
     I've seen it before.

                    MAURICE
     You have?

                    DR. ROYCE
     You're feeling old and you want to
     start exercising. A lot of men
     your age feel the need to recapture
     their youth. Don't feel

embarrassed about it.

                    MAURICE
               (playing along)
          Okay.

                    DR. ROYCE
          You should start slow and easy --
          fifteen minutes a day.

                    MAURICE
          No. How far in one attempt --
          what's the farthest someone like
          myself could walk?

The doctor is confused again.

                    MAURICE
          Just for curiosity sake that's all?

                    DR. ROYCE
          I don't know -- maybe twenty
          miles... Of course I'm not
          recommending that... if someone
          like you had to I mean... that's
          how far they'd probably get before

Walk of Remembrance- Trilogy Part 1

>>encountering serious physical
>>walls.

>>>>MAURICE
>>Twenty miles? I see.

Maurice thinks about it carefully as the doctor returns to the chart.

CUT TO:

INT. AAA AUTO CLUB - DAY

A hip young woman with her forehead wrapped in a headband chews away on a stick of gum. JOSELLE leans over the counter with Maurice and studies a map.

>>>>JOSELLE
>>Each inch represents 150 miles...

>>>>MAURICE
>>Making the grand total?

>>>>JOSELLE
>>Damn baby, relax. I'm getting to
>>>it.
>>>>(taking on a rehearsed
>>>>tone)

Walk of Remembrance- Trilogy Part 1

> From Philadelphia following the
> route highlighted to Pacifica
> California -- you're traveling an
> estimated three thousand two
> hundred miles...

Maurice is a bit pale. He follows the yellow highlighted
highways winding it's way across the U.S.

                MAURICE
Three thousand miles?... How many
times does twenty go into three
thousand?

                JOSELLE
What was that?

                MAURICE
Perhaps there's another route?

                JOSELLE
This is the route approved by
triple A. Even if you followed
back roads the entire way, you'd

                    still be looking at
roughly the
                    same distance...

Joselle studies his concerned
expression.

                         JOSELLE
                    Don't worry baby, it
shouldn't take
                    you more than five days
if you just
                    stop to sleep and eat.

                         MAURICE
                    By car right?

Joselle scrunches her face in
exaggerated shock and takes a
step back to look Maurice up and
down.

                         JOSELLE
                    How else you gonna get
there on the
                    ground?

Maurice gives her a sad expression.
If she only knew.

CUT TO:

INT. NEW STORE - DAY

Walk of Remembrance- Trilogy Part 1

The future Parker Books. The room sits as empty and barren as before.

Maurice sits on the floor against the far wall. He stares at his new store. His gaze turns to the window where the guard strolls by. The guard doesn't notice him.

Maurice looks terrible, his eyes red and framed by bags... his skin a yellowish white.

He moves to his feet and TURNS OFF THE LIGHTS.

CUT TO:

INT. BOOKSTORE - AFTERNOON

Kris unloads the last of a shipment of books. He moves to Maurice who sits by the window to the street. Maurice points to a chair across from him and Kris takes a seat.

> MAURICE
> Why do you want to be a journalist Kris? What sparked your interest?

Walk of Remembrance- Trilogy Part 1

Beat.

                KRIS
I want to reach people. Nobody listens to me. This is my way to reach them.

              MAURICE
To reach people, you have to feel something first... You write about the wrong things. How can you feel for dog food? The people at the Gazette don't respect it, and neither do you.

                KRIS
This is a ghost town. Nothing ever happens.

              MAURICE
Write from your heart. That's why the classics are great.

Beat.

                KRIS

Walk of Remembrance- Trilogy Part 1

    Why are you telling me this Mr.
    Parker?

Maurice looks out the window and picks up an envelope from
the coffee table between them. He hands it to Kris.

      MAURICE
    Your bus is arriving.

Kris opens the envelope and finds money.

      MAURICE
    It's one month's pay.

Kris gets up. A shock of adrenaline hits him.

      KRIS
    Are you firing me?

      MAURICE
    No. No... I won't be here for a
    while. The store will be closed in
    the interim.

Kris grabs his coat, shifting his attention between the
window and Maurice?

      KRIS

Walk of Remembrance- Trilogy Part 1

You going on a trip Mr. Parker?

     MAURICE
Yes.

     KRIS
Where?

     MAURICE
California.

Kris moves to the door.

     KRIS
That's cool. What day are you
  arriving?

Beat.

     MAURICE
I'm not sure -- sometime in January
  I think.

Kris stops cold. The door to the street half-open.

     KRIS
When are you leaving?

     MAURICE
Tomorrow.

Kris is seriously confused now. Maurice decides to end the confusion.

>   MAURICE
>   I'm walking there Kris.

>   KRIS
>   Walking where?

>   MAURICE
>   California.

*Kris' jaw hits the floor as the bus pulls to a stop across
the street. Kris pulls up his sleeve and glances at his
forearm.*

>   KRIS
>   The hairs on my arm are standing
>   up... Something strange is
>   happening.

>   MAURICE
>   I always knew you had good
>   instincts...
>   (beat)
>   Goodbye Kris. I'll see you when I
>   get back.

Walk of Remembrance- Trilogy Part 1

Kris hesitates before darting out of the store, across the street and into the bus. Kris takes a seat in the back and digs into his bag and pulls out the tape recorder. CLICK.

                  KRIS
        Thursday, September 25...
'The
        Death Of A Spouse - Can It Drive
        You Insane?'

CUT TO:

EXT. WYNNEWOOD PENNSYLVANIA - DAWN

A BRILLIANT RED HUE BLANKETS THE HORIZON.

The suburbs come to life...
Men and women leaving for work...
School buses picking up their cargo of passengers...
Store owners opening their businesses...

CUT TO:

PARKER BOOKS

A group of eleven year old boys including the two

Walk of Remembrance- Trilogy Part 1

kleptomaniacs we saw earlier, are standing before a closed door staring at a sign. They look at each other before heading down the block.

The sign reads: CLOSED - OWNER OUT OF TOWN.

CUT TO:

INT. HOUSE - MORNING

The house is eerily silent.

Three things lay on the dining table. A shoulder bag filled with clothes. A carrying bag with personals. And a set of maps.

Maurice checks the locks on all windows... He places all the food in the refrigerator into a trash bag... He pulls out a drawer and loosens a side panel, a wad of money flops out. Maurice pockets the bills...

Maurice walks through the hall with a portable cage. He stops before Claude's hanging cage... no movement, no chirping. Maurice stares emotionally for a moment before

Walk of Remembrance- Trilogy Part 1

reaching in and carefully removing
CLAUDE'S LIFELESS BODY
from the bottom of the cage.
Maurice looks down at the lost
pet in his hands.

                    MAURICE
          I know how you feel.

CUT TO:

EXT. HOUSE - MORNING

Maurice buries the bird in the
backyard.

CUT TO:

DINING ROOM

Maurice sits at the table... the
essentials laying before
him. He clings to a wallet size
photo of Ellen.

Maurice stands and gathers his
things.

CUT TO:

EXT. PENNS LANDING - DAY

*Maurice stands at the edge of the
water. Recreations of
historical ships are docked in the
harbor. The old fashioned
sails and masts sway in the gentle
breeze.*

*The SOUNDS OF A STREET VENDOR catch
Maurice's ears. He turns
to see a funnel cake booth in a row
of food stalls.*

CUT TO:

EXT. TWENTY YEARS EARLIER - DAY
(FLASHBACK)

*The harbor is jammed with people.
A street fair is in full
swing. The SOUNDS OF A LIVE BAND
MIX WITH THE CRIES OF THE
STREET VENDORS...*

*MAURICE -- EARLY TWENTIES...
Skinny, dark rich hair. He
yells out from behind a booth of
paperback books.*

              YOUNG MAURICE
    Three dollars a piece...
Two for
    four dollars! All the
classics!

Walk of Remembrance- Trilogy Part 1

A young woman emerges from the crowd of browsers. Maurice begins to speak but is caught off guard by YOUNG ELLEN'S beautiful features. Maurice manages a few words.

              YOUNG MAURICE
    Can I help you?

Beat.

              YOUNG ELLEN
    My father owns the food stall over
        there.

Maurice looks over to find an enormous man serving food.

              YOUNG ELLEN
    You look thirsty.

Ellen places the soda she had at her side on the table. Maurice is completely flustered.

              YOUNG MAURICE
    Hi, I'm Ellen.

Ellen places her hand out. Maurice grabs it instinctively and shakes.

              YOUNG MAURICE
    Maurice.

Ellen looks at the full table of books.

> YOUNG ELLEN
> Not doing too good huh?

Maurice nods "no."

> YOUNG ELLEN
> It'll pick up. I've been coming to
> these things my whole life...
> people don't want to carry things
> as they walk around... you'll sell
> as the fair starts to end...

Ellen waits for Maurice to say something but nothing comes out.

> YOUNG ELLEN
> You don't talk much do you?

> YOUNG MAURICE
> I read a lot.

Ellen's father BELLOWS FOR HER OVER THE CROWD. Maurice jumps at the sound.

Walk of Remembrance- Trilogy Part 1

                    YOUNG MAURICE
          I better go...
               (Ellen starts for her
               booth)
          ... Come over if you get
hungry.

Ellen disappears into a sea of
people. Maurice stands in awe
for a second before snapping out.
He shakes his head to
himself.

                    YOUNG MAURICE
          I read a lot?

CUT TO:

LATER - IN THE FAIR

The people are filing out of the
street. Maurice is a whirl
wind of activity as people wave
dollar bills at him calling
out classical titles.

Maurice glances over to Ellen's
booth. She is watching him
with a big smile. Maurice gestures
to the line with a
shocked expression. Ellen laughs.

CUT TO:

Walk of Remembrance- Trilogy Part 1

FOOD STALL

*The booths are packing up. Ellen helps pack away the
remaining food. A book is placed in front of her on the
counter. The book is "Romeo and Juliet." Ellen looks up to
see a very shy Maurice standing before her. Ellen gives him
a smile that melts him.*

>   MAURICE
>   Are you trying to tell me
>   something?

*Beat. Maurice eyes Ellen's dad who throws him deadly
glances. Maurice is very intimidated. He whispers to her.*

>   MAURICE
>   (barely audible)
>   Walk with me?

>   ELLEN
>   You like to take walks?

>   MAURICE
>   No. But I want to take a
walk with
>   you.

*Ellen looks at him carefully...
looks right through him.*

Walk of Remembrance- Trilogy Part 1

                    ELLEN
        You just said something very sweet.

CUT TO:

EXT. THE EDGE OF THE WATER - DUSK

The water reflects the lights from the harbor. Maurice and Ellen are standing very close.

                    MAURICE
        What are you thinking?

Ellen looks out onto the water.

                    ELLEN
        It's one of those thoughts you keep
            to yourself.

                    MAURICE
        Please tell me.

Beat.

                    ELLEN
        I was just thinking that if we
            actually became a couple -- this
            was a beautiful place to begin
            things.

*Maurice is bright red. Ellen giggles at his shyness.
Maurice gathers his strength and looks her straight in the eyes.*

Maurice leans forward and kisses her softly.

CUT TO:

EXT. PENNS LANDING - MORNING (PRESENT)

Maurice, tears in his eyes, stands in the spot they stood many years before.

     MAURICE
   (softly)
  I love you Ellen.

On this empty dock... on this hot day in September... with no witnesses and no fan-fare, Maurice Parker takes the first steps of his journey.

SUPERIMPOSED ON THE SCREEN:
SEPTEMBER 26, 1993

CUT TO:

Walk of Remembrance- Trilogy Part 1

EXT. STREET - DAY

A topless CHERRY RED WRANGLER JEEP pulls out of a mechanic's garage and moves down route 32. Kris Reddy is at the wheel. A "Daily Gazette" sign flaps from his roll-bar.

Kris changes the station on the radio as his eye catches a man walking on the opposite side of the street... Kris turns back to the road -- mind racing... BRAKES SCREECH as the jeep slows and then RUMBLES over the island separating the lanes... making a U turn across a four lane highway.

CUT TO:

EXT. STREET - DAY

Maurice wiping his brow with a handkerchief. The Wrangler jeep rolls up next to him as he walks. Maurice doesn't stop walking as Kris leans over the passenger seat.

     KRIS
  Phileas Fogg?

     MAURICE

Walk of Remembrance- Trilogy Part 1

>   *(looking ahead)*
>   ... Round The World In
> Eighty Days.
>   ... Hello Kris.
>
>   KRIS
>   You're amazing... What
> are you
>   doing Mr. Parker?
>
>   MAURICE
>   I told you.

Beat. Cars HONK as they pull by the slow duo.

>   KRIS
>   You're walking to
> California?
>
>   MAURICE
>   Pacifica, California --
> it's a
>   coastal city.
>
>   KRIS
>   Oh, a coastal city.
> That's good.

Kris looks around to see if anyone else sees the lunacy in
this moment.

>   MAURICE
>   Ellen told me that she
> didn't know

Walk of Remembrance- Trilogy Part 1

if I loved her.

                  KRIS
She knew you loved her.

                 MAURICE
She wasn't certain... I never really showed her.

Beat.

                  KRIS
I'm really lost. What does this have to do with walking?

                 MAURICE
I said, 'I would do anything for her'... and she didn't believe me.
I said, 'I'd walk across the country for her'... she didn't believe me.

Maurice looks to Kris rolling along beside him. He sees the worried expression on his face.

                 MAURICE
I need to show her how much I love her Kris.

Walk of Remembrance- Trilogy Part 1

                    KRIS
          Why know?

                    MAURICE
          Because I should have
shown her
          before... Everyday, I
should have
          shown her.

Beat.

                    KRIS
          Pacifica, California...
that's a
          long ways away.

                    MAURICE
          So I've been informed.

Kris tries to act calm, but it
doesn't last long.

                    KRIS
          Shit Mr. Parker. You
can't walk
          across the United States
-- it's
          over three thousand
miles.

Maurice takes his time with the
response. Kris waves more
cars to pass them.

Walk of Remembrance- Trilogy Part 1

                    MAURICE
          Ellen got up every
morning and went
          to the corner store to
get me my
          bread for breakfast...
Everyday.
          Now that's about a
quarter mile
          each way... 17 years...
that comes
          to about three thousand
miles...
               (he smiles to
himself)
          And you know what Kris?

                    KRIS
          What Mr. Parker?

                    MAURICE
          She never ate a slice.

Maurice picks up speed -- surer
with every step... Kris slows
the jeep to a stop and reaches into
his bag. The mini tape
recorder goes on with a CLICK.

                    KRIS
          Thursday, September 26...
'The
          Question We Never Ask -
What Would
          We Do For Love?'

74

Kris watches through the windshield as Mr. Parker disappears down Route 32.

CUT TO:

EXT. PARKER HOUSE - AFTERNOON

The wreaths, flowers and bouquet have now tripled in number. They spill onto the lawn and walkway. A neighborhood dog rummages through the more colorful bouquets.

CUT TO:

INSIDE

The abandoned house. A TELEPHONE RINGS CONTINUOUSLY. It stops after a string of rings. It BEGINS AGAIN AFTER A FEW SECONDS.

CUT TO:

INT. BOOKSTORE - AFTERNOON

The dark bookcases echo the RINGS OF THE TELEPHONE. The answering machine finally picks up.

Walk of Remembrance- Trilogy Part 1

                    MACHINE
(ELLEN'S VOICE)
          Hello you've reached
Parker Books --
          our store hours are eight
to six...

CUT TO:

INT. ADELLE'S HOUSE - AFTERNOON

A center-city Town house. Wall to
wall books, "Cognitive
Psychology", "Physiology of
Behavior", "Abnormal Psychology",
"Clinical Psychology", the titles
cover every shelf and every
tabletop.

Adelle Matlin hangs up the phone,
and moves to the living
room where her husband is reading a
paper in his recliner.

                    ADELLE
          Something's wrong. I'm
worried.

Gerald looks on with an assuring
smile.

                    GERALD
          He probably just went
somewhere.

Walk of Remembrance- Trilogy Part 1

                ADELLE
    Where?

                GERALD
    For a walk. I don't know.

Beat.

                ADELLE
    Uncle Maurice? Are you kidding?
    He hates walking.

CUT TO:

EXT. MOTEL - NIGHT

Nighttime. The empty street ECHOES with the TIRED SHUFFLE OF MAURICE'S FEET.

Maurice stops in this tracks and picks up a CRUSHED COKE CAN FROM THE SIDE OF THE ROAD. He places it upright at the place where he stands. Maurice immediately walks off the highway into a small MOTEL PARKING LOT.

CUT TO:

INT. MOTEL - NIGHT

Walk of Remembrance- Trilogy Part 1

A motel clerk checks his wooden keys.

>   CLERK
>   Pool times are 11 am to 5 pm,
>   there's cable in every room with
>   two premium channels. HBO and
>   CINEMAX. Pay Per View Channels can
>   be --

>   MAURICE
>   I need a bed and I need Tylenol...
>   that's all.

>   CLERK
>   The room comes with two twin Sealy
>   Posturepedics... but the Tylenol
>   will be extra.

Maurice stares at him with exhausted eyes.

CUT TO:

THE INSIDE OF A FLORAL PRINTED ROOM

Maurice's shoulder bags are on the bed... The WATER IS

Walk of Remembrance- Trilogy Part 1

RUNNING IN THE BATHROOM.

Maurice gently moves his hands under the bathtub head, checking the temperature. He sits on the edge of the tub.

Maurice peels off his shoes with great pain. They slide across the dull white tiles into the corner. The once well kept English Loafers could be mistaken for trash now.

Maurice rubs his barefeet with both hands -- grimacing from the pain. The tub is almost filled. Maurice stops the tap. The steam from the water fills the room.

Maurice raises his legs with great effort and submerges each leg into the steaming water. His eyes close with great relief as his body melts into the tub. Maurice lays his head on the side of the tub... It only takes ten seconds before Maurice's SNORING fills the bathroom.

CUT TO:

Walk of Remembrance- Trilogy Part 1

THE OUTSIDE OF THE QUAKER MOTEL ON ROUTE 32

The neon MOTEL SIGN THROBS RED.

SUPERIMPOSED across this image are the words:

*   PHILADELPHIA, PENNSYLVANIA... MILE 26*

CUT TO:

EXT. MOTEL - MORNING

Maurice looks down the highway... eyes squinting to block out the sun. The road winds and dissolves into the horizon... Maurice looks back the way he came -- a second of indecision... the moment passes.

Maurice takes a deep breath before moving to the CRUSHED COKE CAN. He moves to the exact spot where he left the road the night before and begins walking again...

CUT TO:

INT. NEWSPAPER BUILDING - MORNING

Walk of Remembrance- Trilogy Part 1

The elevator BELL dings, letting off a cargo of newspaper personnel. FRANK AND SETH are two of them. They make their way to the desks... a sea of desks pressed against each other -- each desk has a computer.

Frank and Seth come to their corner and stop before a young man, Phillies cap turned backwards, sitting behind an IBM 486 DX... fingers flying over the keyboard.

              FRANK
    Someone's got a hot story.

              SETH
    What time did you get in?

Kris Reddy keeps typing. He spits out the answer after a few seconds.

              KRIS
    Five... Couldn't sleep.

              FRANK
    What's this one about Kris?
    'Blinds or Curtains - The Eternal
    Question?'

Walk of Remembrance- Trilogy Part 1

                    SETH
          No, no... 'Boxers Verses
Tight
          Undies - The Battle
Continues.'

Frank and Seth crack up laughing.
Frank reaches for the
printouts... Kris immediately
covers them with his hand. He
stares up with a smile.

                    KRIS
          Read about it on Sunday.

CUT TO:

EXT. STREET - DAY

Maurice exits an athletic store in
a small town. On his feet
a new pair of sneakers.

CUT TO:

EXT. STREET - DAY

Maurice as he walks down a winding
highway. His new sneakers
shuffling slowly.

A SHARP PAIN SHOOTS UP MAURICE'S
LEG. His knees buckle. The

Walk of Remembrance- Trilogy Part 1

shoulder bags tumble to the ground followed by Maurice
himself. From a distance it looks like he's been shot.

Maurice grabs the back of his thigh and tries to straighten
his leg out... His face frozen in a painful expression.
Maurice rubs his legs slowly -- working the cramp out. He
relaxes a bit as he finally straightens his leg. Maurice
sits there motionless -- eyes glazed... defeated.

The SOUNDS OF A BIRD snap him out of his trance. He looks up
to see a PAINTED BUNTING, a bird about six inches in height
FLY DOWN from a tree and land on a rock next to him. Maurice
stares at the beautiful bird curiously. Its body splashed
with brilliant blues, reds and greens. It looks out of place
in these mundane surroundings. Maurice looks around the
skies to see no other birds. The Painted Bunting chirps a
few times before taking flight into the air. It circles over
Maurice before disappearing behind the trees.

Walk of Remembrance- Trilogy Part 1

Maurice smiles. He pulls himself to his feet with great effort.

Maurice opens all of his bags and begins emptying the essentials -- the maps, food, a canister of water.

Maurice reloads one bag and pulls it over his shoulder with great effort. At his feet, are the rest of his belonging -- piled on the side of the road.

Maurice painfully begins walking again.

WE PULL BACK on Maurice's figure walking on the highway... the pile of disregarded things laying by the side... The highway is endless... winding it's way for miles and miles into a fixed dot in the distance.

CUT TO:

INT. ADELLE'S HOUSE - MORNING

Sunrise on Pennsylvania. Gerald picks the Philadelphia Gazette off the front porch.

Walk of Remembrance- Trilogy Part 1

CUT TO:

DINING ROOM

Gerald flips open the paper as he waits before an empty plate.

                    GERALD
     Smells good, honey.

CUT TO:

KITCHEN

Adelle puts the finishing touches on a stack of pancakes.
She sets up two plates and brings them into the

DINING ROOM

Gerald's eyes remain glued to the paper. Adelle comes to the table, holding the golden pancakes over the table. She notices the strange look on his face.

                    ADELLE
     What is it?

                    GERALD

Walk of Remembrance- Trilogy Part 1

Adelle... Maurice is in the paper.

She stares silently at the paper laid out on the table. The headline beams at her:

A PHILADELPHIA NATIVE'S LABOR OF LOVE

Adelle is shocked. She gazes at an old picture of her uncle printed underneath the headline.

ADELLE
Oh my God.

She STORMS off into the kitchen with the golden pancakes. Gerald looks down at his empty plate longingly.

GERALD
Honey.

CUT TO:

INT. POLICE STATION - DAY

SERGEANT DALLY pretends to be concerned.

DALLY
What would you like us to do?

Walk of Remembrance- Trilogy Part 1

>   ADELLE
>   Put out a P.B.S.... Or whatever
>   it's called.
>
>   DALLY
>   A.P.B.... He isn't breaking any
>   law. He's a grown man... He can
>   crawl on his hands and knees to
>   China if that's what he wants to
>   do.
>
>   ADELLE
>   Sergeant, I'm a psychologist and I
>   know the difference between normal
>   whims people have and actions that
>   clearly display psychological
>   problems... My uncle lost his wife
>   and it devastated him.
>
>   DALLY
>   We're very sorry about that. Some
>   of our men were on the scene of the
>   accident.

Walk of Remembrance- Trilogy Part 1

>   ADELLE
> I think my uncle is suffering from
> a condition called Mania which is
> linked with depression. It is a
> time when an individual will act
> over-confident, and will act out
> impractical, grandiose plans.
> Sometimes these plans can be
> dangerous.

>   DALLY
> How long does this... Mania last?

>   ADELLE
> A couple days to a few months if
> untreated.

Dally digests this information.

>   DALLY
> Look, I'll see if anyone has
> spotted him recently. If I get any
> information, I'll call you.

					ADELLE
			Thank you.

					DALLY
			Don't wait by the phone.
If he's
			really been walking this
whole
			time, he's out of our
			jurisdiction...

Adelle looks very emotional... on
the verge of tears.

					DALLY
			Don't worry he'll be
back. He's in
			his forties. He's had no
physical
			training... He'll be back
by the
			end of the week.

CUT TO:

EXT. HIGHWAYS - DAY

A floating DOT moves along a flat
stretch of road...

DISSOLVE TO:

EVENING

Walk of Remembrance- Trilogy Part 1

The sun drops behind rolling hills.
The DOT has become
LARGER, sprouting arms and legs...

DISSOLVE TO:

NIGHT

Darkness has fallen. The DOT has materializes into MAURICE.

CUT TO:

MOTEL

A clerk hands over a set of keys in exchange for money.

DISSOLVE TO:

ROAD - MORNING

Maurice walks back onto the highway and steps next to an old boot that has been used as today's MARKER. Maurice starts walking from that point.

DISSOLVE TO:

DRUGSTORE

Walk of Remembrance- Trilogy Part 1

Maurice grabs two handfuls of small green boxes. He places them on the table. The cashier stares down at the eight boxes of Ben-Gay and rings it up.

DISSOLVE TO:

ROAD

Maurice standing at the entrance to a tunnel that pierces the side of a mountain side. Maurice makes "The sign of the cross" and walks into the darkness...

DISSOLVE TO:

EXIT OF TUNNEL

Maurice appears on the other side with a smile of relief. He's awed at the beauty of the landscape. Tiny clusters of buildings far in the distance wrapped in a blanket of green for miles on every side.

DISSOLVE TO:

MOTEL

Walk of Remembrance- Trilogy Part 1

Maurice asleep in the bathtub.

DISSOLVE TO:

ROAD - DUSK

It's raining hard like gun-fire from the sky. Maurice sits on the edge of a road rubbing his legs. His hair matted to his head. The rain pelts the ground in forceful waves.

DISSOLVE TO:

SUPPLY STORE

At a cash register, Maurice slaps ten more boxes of Ben-Gay down on the counter. A teenage girl with braces looks at him like he's Charles Manson.

DISSOLVE TO:

MOTEL

Maurice sleeps. His barefeet are propped up on his bag. His feet are swollen and red with fresh blisters. A pack of ice

Walk of Remembrance- Trilogy Part 1

is wrapped around his knee with an old shirt... The picture of Ellen clutched in his hand.

DISSOLVE TO:

ROAD

*Two joggers pass Maurice as he sees a flashing school sign.
It is a suburban town. The fallen red and orange leaves
cover every flat surface.*

SUPERIMPOSE: ELKHART, INDIANA... MILE 598

CUT TO:

EXT. SCHOOL - DAY

A line of cars pulls around a semi-circle driveway. Maurice watches as parents drop off their children. A couple of ten year old boys walk by.

      BOY
  Nice sneaks.

Maurice realizes they're talking to him.

      MAURICE

Walk of Remembrance- Trilogy Part 1

>   *They are?*
>
>   BOY 2
>   *Sure man, High-Top Nike Cross*
>   *Trainers with heel supports and air*
>   *cushioned soles --*
> *They're nasty.*

The boys keep walking. Maurice looks down at his sneakers with new-found pride.

After a while, Maurice's attention switches back to the cars. One car in question catches Maurice's eye. A woman consoles a small child who doesn't want to leave the car. She wipes his tiny tears with her hand and hugs him tenderly. The little boy's head cradled in her arms.

CUT TO:

EXT. FIFTEEN YEARS AGO - NIGHT (FLASHBACK)

The Parker house many years ago. The house semi-furnished. Ellen carefully hangs her first bird photographs on the wall;

Walk of Remembrance- Trilogy Part 1

a striking aerial photo of a GOLDEN EAGLE. Wings spread,
soaring high over a mountain range.

                MAURICE
      I thought we both wanted the same
          things.

                ELLEN
      I've changed my mind.

                MAURICE
      You can't change your mind.

Beat. Ellen takes a seat on the only sofa.

                ELLEN
      I want children.

                MAURICE
      You've just decided, is that right?

                ELLEN
      Yes.

Young Maurice is visibly upset.

                MAURICE
      Ellen, there are two kinds of
          people in the world --

Walk of Remembrance- Trilogy Part 1

                    ELLEN
          Please not, 'The two kinds of
          people' speech.

                    MAURICE
          ... People that were made to be
          parents, and people who were not
          made to be parents... My parents,
          were people who were not made to be
          parents but had kids anyway. I
          don't want us to be that way Ellen.

                    ELLEN
          You can change.

                    MAURICE
          Face it Ellen, I'm not the type of
          person who reads bedtime stories.
          But you love me anyway.

                    ELLEN
               (upset)
          Don't be so sure.

Ellen fiddles with her dress. She bites her bottom lip as
she tries not to cry.

Walk of Remembrance- Trilogy Part 1

                    ELLEN
              (shaky voice)
        What if something happens to one of
        us? We'll be all alone.

Maurice loses his hard demeanor and moves next to her. He
lays his hand across her shoulder.

                    MAURICE
        Nothing will happen to us. It's a
        bleak picture, I know, but we're
        going to be together till were old
        and grey and you don't remember my
        name anymore.

Maurice lifts her chin with his hand gently. She blinks her
eyes and a tear rolls down her cheek. He takes a deep
breath.

                    MAURICE
        Let me think about it okay.

Ellen brightens up immediately.

                    MAURICE

Walk of Remembrance- Trilogy Part 1

              I'm not saying anytime soon. I'm
                  just saying that maybe we can
                  consider it down the road sometime.

Ellen gives her patented glowing smile. She hugs him with
all her strength. She whispers in his ear.

                      ELLEN
           I love you Maurice Parker.

CUT TO:

EXT. INDIANA GRADE SCHOOL - DAY (PRESENT)

Maurice walks away from the school, shuffling through the
piles of leaves that block the walkways.

A child and her father walk down the path towards him.
Maurice looks away painfully. THE CHILD'S SOFT LAUGHTER
POUNDING IN HIS EARS as he quickens his pace.

CUT TO:

Walk of Remembrance- Trilogy Part 1

INT. LIQUOR STORE - DAY

JACKSON LIQUOR WHOLESALERS. For the kind of people who buy whiskey by the crate.

Maurice has his map unfolded over the cash register.

                    CASHIER
     I can show you the main roads, but
     that'll add ten miles to your trip.
     Do you mind ten miles?

                    MAURICE
     I mind.

CUT TO:

OUTSIDE OF LIQUOR STORE

The parking lot of the store looks like a used truck lot.
Every kind of supped-up truck one could possibly imagine is
on display here.

Maurice passes a CANARY YELLOW FLATBED PICK-UP with a group of men drinking a newly purchased case of beer. Maurice gets

Walk of Remembrance- Trilogy Part 1

about ten feet past them when he
stops, hesitates and then
heads back to them.

                    MAURICE
          Excuse me, who's truck is
this?

The man sitting on the hood of the
truck, has dark hair and
hasn't shaven in days. This
unfortunate gentleman is named
DENNY.

                    DENNY
          Mine.

                    MAURICE
          Are you and your friends
planning
          on driving soon?

Denny gives Maurice a greasy
curious look. He squints his
glazed eyes.

                    DENNY
          Yes we are. Who the fuck
are you?

Maurice, doesn't look scared, in
fact he looks angered.

                    MAURICE
          You don't know me from
Adam, but I

>   want you to do something for me. I
>   want you to wait until you sobered
>   up before you get behind the wheel.
>   I know this is out of the ordinary,
>   but one man to another, would you
>   do me that favor?

Silence. Then everyone in the group BURSTS OUT IN DRUNKEN LAUGHTER.

>   DENNY
>   Are you a preacher?

>   MAURICE
>   (seething with anger)
>   No, I just don't want anybody dying
>   because I didn't say something when
>   I had the chance.

Denny's face goes blank. No emotion. His steady gaze almost terrifying.

>   DENNY
>   I'll drive my truck shit-faced if I
>   want to. You better turn around

> and walk away preacher. You don't
> know who you're talking to.

Maurice looks around at the hostile faces and decides on a
retreat. Denny watches Maurice with predatory eyes.

CUT TO:

EXT. ROAD - DUSK

Maurice practically hobbles his way down a road lined by
towering pines. He stops to take a drink from his canister
and keeps walking. The SOUNDS OF A CAR GROW IN THE DISTANCE.
Maurice doesn't turn his back.

The CANARY YELLOW TRUCK pulls over the ridge with a load full
of passengers. It gains distance on Maurice.

Maurice hears the ENGINE and waves HIS ARM IN THE AIR --
signaling for it to pass him. Maurice walks ten more feet
before turning around.

Maurice's face instantly changes when he sees the demented

grins through the windshield of the truck. Maurice turns and quickens his pace... The truck picks up pace... Maurice breaks into a run... The truck speeds up, passes Maurice and stops in front of him.

Panic fills Maurice as he watches the truck unload it's drunken passengers. Eyes scan the forest on either side for a way out. Maurice decides to stand his ground.

                MAURICE
        (to himself)
    This is Indiana -- nothing's going
    to happen to you.

                DENNY
    You need a ride, Preacher?

The men walk up to Maurice.

                MAURICE
    No thank you I'll walk.

A tall lanky gentleman gestures to Maurice's shoulder bag with his beer can. Some beer sprays Maurice's feet with the gesture.

Walk of Remembrance- Trilogy Part 1

> WIL
> Where you coming from?

> MAURICE
> Look gentlemen, I'm late, I need to --

> DENNY
> I've been thinking -- who the hell is this preacher guy? Coming up to me and my friends? Looking like he wanted to kick my ass for drinking?

Denny gives Maurice that inhuman stare. Maurice is clearly frightened.

> DENNY
> Then I figured it. You're angry. You lost somebody, because some asshole was drinking.

Maurice is frozen.

> DENNY
> Maybe you lost a son? A sister? A wife?

Walk of Remembrance- Trilogy Part 1

Maurice looks up for a millisecond. Denny doesn't miss it.

                    DENNY
              (stepping closer)
     A wife?... Did someone piss drunk
     run into your wife? Crushed her
     like a bug. Snapped her bones?

                    MAURICE
     That's enough.

Maurice is red with anger. Denny loves it.

                    DENNY
     Oh the preacher's getting angry
     again...
        (Denny goes ice cold)
     Tell me something. Did she die
     instantly or did she feel every
     torn muscle and shattered bone?
     Were you there to help her? Or
     were you safe at home when the
     windshield sliced into her face --

Walk of Remembrance- Trilogy Part 1

                    MAURICE
          I'll kill you!

Maurice swings. Denny easily
avoids it. Maurice doesn't see
the first BLOW COMING, IT HITS HIM
IN THE CHEST -- Maurice
gasps for air as he buckles to the
dirt. Hands grab --
restrain. A POWERFUL KICK IN THE
RIBS -- ANOTHER...
LAUGHTER... ANOTHER SET OF VICIOUS
KICKS... The road and
forest begin to spin... A PAINFUL
SLASH ACROSS HIS FACE...

Maurice prepares for the next
blow... it never comes. RED
AND BLUE lights swirl... Maurice
looks up, barely focusing --
a man leans over a car door... The
image becomes clearer -- a
POLICEMAN stands poised -- gun
aimed directly at the men
hovering over him.

                    POLICE OFFICER
               (distorted and
slowed)
          Step away from him now!

CUT TO:

INT. INDIANA POLICE STATION -
EVENING

Walk of Remembrance- Trilogy Part 1

OFFICER MERRIL GREY -- balances a phone on his shoulder as he spreads a new coat of mayonnaise on his hoagie.

                OFFICER GREY
    Need an I.D. check on a Maurice A.
    Parker...

Grey reads Maurice's license.

                OFFICER GREY
    Driver's number 22 184 877...
        (listening)
    He was assaulted by a group of men
    just outside Elkhart, Indiana...

CUT TO:

INT. PHILADELPHIA POLICE STATION - EVENING

Sergeant Dally, the officer Adelle spoke to earlier, listens
on the other end of the phone his mouth agape.

                DALLY
    How is he?... That's good.

Walk of Remembrance- Trilogy Part 1

*Gesturing to a young officer at another desk to come over.
Dally, cups the phone.*

                  DALLY
    Call Adelle Matlin...
tell her we
      found her uncle.

CUT TO:

INT. PHILADELPHIA GAZETTE BUILDING - EVENING

The sea of desks are empty. One empty desk is lit -- Kris Reddy's desk. THE CRACKLE OF A SHORTWAVE/C.B. UNIT FLOATS THROUGH THE LARGE UNOCCUPIED ROOM *from an adjacent room. The* VOICES OF DALLY AND OFFICER GREY ARE DISTORTED BUT AUDIBLE.

WE MOVE TO the back room to find Kris writing furiously in front of an elaborate C.B. setup.

He jots down the words as fast as they're said:

  "Maurice Parker... Elkhart... Route 80... Precinct 18..."

Walk of Remembrance- Trilogy Part 1

*The transmission gets cut as the
phone conversation ends.
Kris quickly rolls the chair across
the room and grabs a map
off the shelf.*

*The map gets pinned under two
coffee cups and a ceramic frog
as Kris traces the route from
Philadelphia to Indiana... He
sits up straight in astonishment as
his eyes hit the KEY of
the map.*

                    KRIS
        *Jesus -- he's walked six hundred
        miles.*

*Kris glances at the hairs on his
arm and smiles.*

CUT TO:

LATER

*Kris at his computer and in the
'zone.' Fingers flying over
the keys passionately. On his desk
is a cardboard box filled
with letters all shapes and sizes
on the verge of overflowing
the top of the box. One the side
of the box are the words,
"Labor of Love - Fan Mail."*

Walk of Remembrance- Trilogy Part 1

CUT TO:

INT. INDIANA POLICE STATION - MORNING

DAWN IN INDIANA -- the sun spills over the horizon.

CUT TO:

EXT. INDIANA POLICE STATION - MORNING

Maurice and Officer Grey are seated on the front stairs of the precinct drinking coffee when ADELLE MATLIN DRIVES UP.

Adelle steps out of a RENTED TOYOTA CELICA. Her tense -- frightened eyes betray her mental state for the past ten hours. She walks to the stairs.

              GREY
    Mrs. Matlin... good morning.

Maurice slowly gets up. Adelle is in shock as she looks at the stranger before her.

Walk of Remembrance- Trilogy Part 1

Maurice stands in a 'COLTS' football T-shirt, faded jeans and sneakers. His left cheek is black and blue, and his arm and side are bandaged.

                  ADELLE
     Uncle Maurice, you're wearing
     sneakers?

                  MAURICE
     High-top Nike Cross-Trainers with
     heel support and air-cushioned
     soles. They're nasty.

Adelle wasn't sure what that meant. She shakes it off and hugs Maurice. She is visibly relieved to have him in her arms.

                  GREY
     My shift ended an hour ago.

Adelle notices the ROSE in Grey's hand. Grey catches her glance.

                  GREY
     It's for my wife.

                  ADELLE

Walk of Remembrance- Trilogy Part 1

>   *What's the occasion?*

Grey looks to Maurice -- they exchange a knowing smile.

>   GREY
>   No occasion.

Adelle notices the WINK exchanged between Grey and Maurice.

>   GREY
>   You can use the
>   conference room, if
>   you want to talk.

>   ADELLE
>   That won't be necessary.

>   GREY
>   Fine.

>   ADELLE
>   We can talk on the way
>   back -- I
>   rented a car.

Beat.

>   MAURICE
>   It'll be kind of hard to
>   talk,
>   since you'll be in the
>   car and I
>   won't.

Adelle gives Maurice an angry glare -- Maurice holds his ground.

                    GREY
         The conference room is down the
         hall on your right.

CUT TO:

INT. POLICE CONFERENCE ROOM - MORNING

File cabinets in the corners. A small rectangle table takes up ninety percent of the space in the room.

Maurice is seated -- his legs extended straight on another chair. Adelle paces the front of the room.

                   ADELLE
         And your store? What about your
         new store? What about all your
         dreams?

                   MAURICE
         I have new dreams now.

                   ADELLE

Walk of Remembrance- Trilogy Part 1

    I don't accept that.

      MAURICE
    Maybe one day -- after you've been
    married twenty years you'll
    understand.

      ADELLE
    Uncle Maurice -- I spent all our
    frequent flyer miles on a one way
    ticket here... I have a rented car
    outside, just listen to me.
      (beat)
    Come back with me now, and if you
    still want to do something like
    this in a year -- maybe we'll plan
    a car trip across the country --
    Gerald and I will come along --

      MAURICE
    I have to walk -- by myself -- all
    the way -- every inch.

      ADELLE

It's impossible.

MAURICE
It's what she asked for... It's
what I'm going to do.

ADELLE
She was being symbolic. What if
she asked you to fly to the moon?

MAURICE
You'd be visiting me at Nasa.

Adelle changes gears. She takes a seat next to Maurice and studies his legs and tired face carefully before uttering the words.

ADELLE
(whispering)
What if you don't make it?

MAURICE
I'll make it.

ADELLE
If you really want to do this...
plan it out. Rest up. Train for

Walk of Remembrance- Trilogy Part 1

     it. Build up your body. Plan
     every stop along the way. How much
     money? Time? Really do it
     properly. This is all so -- by the
     seat of your pants.

       MAURICE
     No it's not.

       ADELLE
     Why did you take the back roads
     here? They're not safe. You'd
     know that if you'd planned.

Beat.

       MAURICE
     I've all ready gone six hundred
     miles... I can't do it again.

       ADELLE
     If you can't redo these six hundred
     miles when you're rested and ready,
     how are you possible going to walk

Walk of Remembrance- Trilogy Part 1

                    another two thousand-five hundred
           miles in your present condition?

Maurice is stumped. He looks unsure. He instantly looks on the verge of tears.

                    MAURICE
          Nothing's going to happen.

                    ADELLE
          Uncle, the way I was told, if that
          police car didn't happen down that
          road, you would be dead right now.
          That guy Denny, had jumped bail in
          another state, he's dangerous...
          They'll be other Dennys, if you
          don't plan.

Maurice stares down at the table -- the life draining from him with every word she says.

                    ADELLE
          Ellen, deserves you to do this

Walk of Remembrance- Trilogy Part 1

                    right. Really make it --
if you're
          going to do it. She
deserves it.

CUT TO:

INT. CAR - DAY

The RENTED TOYOTA CELICA turns out
of the police station onto
the main road.

Adelle holds a cushion in the air
as she looks in the
rearview mirror.

                         ADELLE
          Do you want this? It's a
long
          ride.

Maurice is stretched out in the
back -- his legs propped up
on a blanket. Maurice shakes his
head "no" silently.

His sad eyes watching the passing
scenery. The speeding car
swallows up the miles effortlessly.
Maurice watches the
Jackson Liquor Wholesalers whiz
by... The painful hills he
climbed, gone, in an instant... The
school where he watched

the children being dropped off, swishes by in a blink... all those miles lost.

Maurice shuts his eyes in pain.

CUT TO:

EXT. GAS STATION/REST STOP - DAY

The rented Toyota Celica is parked at the convenience store. Maurice is seated in the back staring out at the eighteen wheelers that come in and out of the parking lot. He glances in to Adelle who is gathering food.

Maurice's dull eyes are about to shut when something catches his attention. He sits up and stares out the window with great intensity. Maurice watches as a large truck pulls into the parking lot, across it's side in blazing red --

"Jackson Liquor Wholesalers - Since 1945"

Maurice scans the area... gas station ATTENDANTS... A BEARDED HOMELESS MAN laying next to a heating unit... KIDS eating fast food on old picnic tables...

Walk of Remembrance- Trilogy Part 1

Maurice's gaze steadies on the TRUCK, as the driver fills the tank with gas.

CUT TO:

A PHONE BOOTH INSIDE THE CONVENIENCE STORE

Adelle is on the phone.

              ADELLE
We'll figure everything out when we get there... Oh, he's going to need a lot of help with this... He wasn't even going to come with me, I had to tell him that he could do the walk later if he plans well... I know, but by that time I'll have gotten him some treatment... I just want to get back home before he changes his mind.

CUT TO:

Walk of Remembrance- Trilogy Part 1

CAR - LATER

Adelle gets in the front seat of the car keeping the bag of food on the passenger seat. She starts the car as she talks into the rearview mirror.

> ADELLE
> You want something to eat?

She stares at Maurice covered in a blanket with his back to her... an unresponsive blob.

> ADELLE
> I know you're feeling a lot of emotions right now. It's okay to be mad. It's okay to feel helpless. It's part of the healing process. I understand. I do.

Adelle puts the Celica into drive and pulls out onto the highway.

DISSOLVE TO:

Walk of Remembrance- Trilogy Part 1

EXT. ADELLE'S HOUSE - EVENING

Evening in Philadelphia. The rented Toyota Celica pulls into the driveway. The front door of the house opens. Gerald walks out to greet them.

A tired Adelle slips out of the car and hugs Gerald.

                  ADELLE
    He was exhausted -- slept the whole
        way.

Adelle and Gerald move to the back door of the Celica. They open it and stare at Maurice covered by the blanket. Adelle shakes the blanket.

                  ADELLE
    Uncle Maurice we're home... Uncle
        Maurice.

Adelle shakes Maurice, who stirs a little as he wakes. His feet slide out from under the blanket -- Adelle stares curiously at the ARMY COMBAT BOOTS that dangle out.

                  ADELLE
    Uncle Maurice?

Walk of Remembrance- Trilogy Part 1

*Adelle pulls aside the covers...
THE HOMELESS MAN, from the
gas station, sits up. ADELLE'S
SHRILL SCREAM BLASTS THROUGH
THE AIR. Gerald and Adelle stumble
back as the large,
bearded man struggles out of the
car and looks around the
quiet neighborhood.*

>   HOMELESS MAN
>   So this is the City of
> Brotherly
>   Love.

*The homeless man raises his hand.
He holds up MAURICE'S WELL
POLISHED BOOK SOCIETY MEDALLION and
kisses it lovingly.*

*Adelle and Gerald stare back
speechless.*

DISSOLVE TO:

EXT. ROAD - MORNING

*JACKSON WHOLESALER'S PARKING LOT.
The truck from the gas
station, the only vehicle parked
before the store.*

CUT TO:

Walk of Remembrance- Trilogy Part 1

EXT.   ROAD - MORNING

Maurice back on the road. His limp only slightly visible at
this point in the day. The bandages rubbing him with every
step.

The highway takes him around a beautiful bend of trees. THE
AIR IS FILLED WITH THE SOUNDS OF BIRDS. Maurice spots a
YELLOW WARBLER, a striking bird about eight inches long with
vivid yellow feathers. It sits elegantly on a nearby branch.
He walks towards it -- it stays in position. Closer. The
bird chirps back at him. Maurice is within arms reach of the
bird.

                    MAURICE
        Ellen would have loved you.

Maurice looks closer -- and notices it's wings. The feathers
bend back -- a dark area at the center.

                    MAURICE
        How did that happen?

Maurice watches the bird hop around the branch -- unable to fly.

CUT TO:

INT. PARKER KITCHEN - FIFTEEN YEARS EARLIER (FLASHBACK)

The kitchen is a different color. The refrigerator and appliances are brand new. Ellen walks in -- something cradled in her hand. Maurice looks up from his paper to see Ellen move to the sink and lay a motionless bird on the counter.

          ELLEN
      (shaky voice)
  It must've hit the window... I
  think its neck is broken.

          MAURICE
  Don't bring it in here -- it
  probably has all kinds of diseases.

Ellen finds an eye dropper from the table and fills it with water -- she lets a few drops fall into the birds mouth.

Walk of Remembrance- Trilogy Part 1

CUT TO:

BEDROOM

Evening, just before bed. Maurice is reading. Ellen is monitoring the bird closely. It lays on the bedside table -- wrapped gently with a hand towel. A morsel of food is lowered into its mouth with a pair of tweezers. The bird stares blankly at the ceiling.

          MAURICE
  It isn't going to make it Ellen.
   Let the poor thing go quietly.

          ELLEN
  It'll make it.

Her delicate hand rubs the bird's stomach.

CUT TO:

LIVING ROOM

The GRAPHIC IMAGES of the TV FLICKER on Maurice's face. He

Walk of Remembrance- Trilogy Part 1

glances back to Ellen who talks to the bird cradled in her arms.

>   ELLEN
>   (softly)
>   You must miss flying. Being way up
>   there in the clouds looking down at
>   all of us. You miss that don't
>   you? You miss playing with your
>   friends and talking with them...

In the SOFT LIGHT of the lamp -- Ellen has transformed into a mother rocking her child to sleep.

CUT TO:

KITCHEN

Maurice is reading his paper.

>   ELLEN
>   Maurice! Maurice! Come out here.

Maurice looks through the window to see Ellen waving to him frantically.

Walk of Remembrance- Trilogy Part 1

CUT TO:

BACKYARD

Ellen points to the ground. The little bird awkwardly walks around the porch.

The bird's wings BURST into motion -- flapping hard -- catching the wind. Ellen jumps up and down, bursting with pride, as her little child takes flight.

                    MAURICE
    I don't believe it.

Ellen hugs Maurice.

                    ELLEN
    All he needed was love. Once you
    have that, you can do anything.

Young Maurice and Ellen watch the bird soar into the blue sky.

CUT TO:

EXT. STREAM - DAY (PRESENT)

Walk of Remembrance- Trilogy Part 1

Maurice is kneeling at a stream by the side of the road. He gently clears away the dirt from the Yellow Warbler's feathers.

> MAURICE
> You'll be all right. A couple days
> and you'll be up there again.

Maurice carries the bird back to the trees. He lays it back on the branch. He stares at it's beautiful coat with a smile.

> MAURICE
> Ellen would have loved you.

CUT TO:

INT. ADELLE'S KITCHEN - DAY

Adelle is on the cordless. Her fingers tapping on the kitchen table angrily. Gerald moves around her as he sets two plates at the table.

> ADELLE
> Yes I understand, it does sound

Walk of Remembrance- Trilogy Part 1

humorous, but this is a very serious situation.

Gerald is cooking. He gently flips the chicken breast in a butter and garlic sauce.

                GERALD
This smells good.

                ADELLE
Why am I such an authority?

                GERALD
        (under his breath)
Here comes the resume.

                ADELLE
I received my B.S. from the University of Pennsylvania, my P.H.D. from Bryn Mawr College. I worked three years at the Boston University School of Medicine, during which time I had articles printed in the "Journal of Educational Psychology", "American

Journal of Psychology",
"Psychology
Review" and "Science"...
So I think
it's safe to say my
opinion is
valid.

Gerald brings the sizzling pan over and divides the steaming dish into both plates.

                    ADELLE
Look, please find him for
me...
Officer, I tried... but I
brought
back the wrong person.

Gerald quickly scoops some rice onto both plates. His mouth is watering as he goes for the utensils.

Adelle abruptly stands at her place.

                    ADELLE
Stop laughing!

Gerald gets into his seat at the table just in time to see Adelle angrily hang up the phone. She stares off into space before unconsciously cleaning the table. Adelle picks up

Walk of Remembrance- Trilogy Part 1

both plates of food...

                GERALD
      Adelle --

Gerald's heart sinks as Adelle pops open the trash can with a tap of her foot and dumps the picture perfect meal into the garbage. She goes to the sink and rinses the plates completely preoccupied with her thoughts. She mumbles to herself as she shuts off the water.

                ADELLE
      He says he admires him.

Adelle storms out of the kitchen. Gerald sits at the empty table with a fork in his hands. He shakes his head in disbelief.

CUT TO:

EXT. MIDWEST HIGHWAYS - DAY

The land is flat. From the roads one can see endless fields in all directions. When the wind blows, the crops bend in unison, changing the shape and texture of the land for a

Walk of Remembrance- Trilogy Part 1

moment and instantly changing back with a snap of the wind.

Maurice takes in the beauty of the land through a painful grimace. Occasionally clutching his right leg in moments of extreme pain.

Maurice rests on an abandoned tractor by the side of the road and watches the wind change the fields. He closes his jacket as the gusts become stronger.

DISSOLVE TO:

HOTEL

The clock clicks past 11:30 am. Maurice is still in bed -- the curtains drawn. He crawls out from under the sheets and downs two pills with a glass of water. He looks bad. His face pale, his eyes at half-mast. He wipes unnatural sweat from his brow and melts into the bed again.

DISSOLVE TO:

STREET

Walk of Remembrance- Trilogy Part 1

Just after dusk. A small town's main road. Maurice quietly passes under the street lights.

He stares up and tightens the hood on his parka as the first SNOWFLAKE falls into the SHAFT OF THE STREET LIGHT. Soon thousands of flakes fall into the light...

DISSOLVE TO:

GAZETTE BUILDING

Kris fields calls frantically as the LIGHTS BLINK ANXIOUSLY on his phone. The front page of the Gazette is posted on his pin up board. It reads... "HE MARCHES ON..." Underneath is A PICTURE of Maurice standing outside his bookstore holding up THE BOOK SOCIETY MEDALLION proudly.

A teenage boy gets off the elevator and maneuvers an enormous bag over his shoulder... emblazoned across his back are the words "MAIL ROOM." The boy comes to Kris and empties the bag on Kris' desk without a word. Hundreds of letters cascade

Walk of Remembrance- Trilogy Part 1

down swallowing the table top and covering Kris who stares in awe as the letters keep coming.

DISSOLVE TO:

MOTEL

Maurice is COUGHING PAINFULLY. He crouches over the edge of the bed and holds his side with every strain.

Maurice looks worse than ever. His hair and shirt are soaked with sweat. The coughing attack stops. Maurice take a couple deep breaths before laying back down.

His feet are visible -- sticking out from beneath the sheets. They look like someone has beaten them with a stick, swollen and bruised. They disappear under the sheets.

DISSOLVE TO:

SNOW COVERED ROADS

that stretch into a white oblivion.

Walk of Remembrance- Trilogy Part 1

SUPERIMPOSE: ELM CREEK,
NEBRASKA... MILE 1,564

CUT TO:

EXT. STREET - DAY

Early morning. The branches of the trees are encapsulated in
ice. The snow piled ten inches on every surface. Maurice,
buried deep beneath three layers of clothes, looks around.
His breath materializes with every step. He forces a weak
smile at the magical landscape before him. White. Pure.
Peaceful.

The SOUNDS OF A VOLVO STATION WAGON urges Maurice to the side
of the road. As it passes a little girl waves from the
passenger window. Maurice puts on a brave face and waves
back.

Another CAR ENTERS the picture -- A DARK BLUE FIREBIRD rises
over the hill in the opposite lane moving fast, too fast.

SLOW-MOTION as the Firebird skids over the ice and the snow

Walk of Remembrance- Trilogy Part 1

-- the driver desperately trying to gain control... The mother in the Volvo hits the BRAKES as the Firebird spins into her lane... Maurice yells out.

                    MAURICE
        No!

The cars IMPACT with a sickening CRUNCH -- BACK TO REAL TIME:

The Firebird spins into a guardrail, breaking through it and coming to a stop in a bank of snow.

The Volvo isn't so lucky. It flips from the impact... sliding on its roof, driving through the snow, down the road... It comes to a rest a hundred feet away.

SILENCE. STILLNESS. The entire event took only seconds.

Maurice runs frantically after the Volvo. The windows are SHATTERED. Snow has packed into the over-turned car. No one can be seen inside the vehicle.

Maurice kneels down and punctures the wall of snow with his hand. His arm disappears up to the shoulder. His face

Walk of Remembrance- Trilogy Part 1

grimacing with the strain. His arm comes out slowly...

A few MUFFLED SOBS ARE HEARD BEFORE the little girl breaks through the wall of snow and slides out of the window. She lets out a DESPERATE GASP for air as Maurice pulls her out by the wrist.

Maurice clears her mouth and face and watches as she coughs.

                MAURICE
          (panting)
     It's okay. It's all over.

Maurice lays her gently against a snow bank, before moving to the other side of the car.

                DRIVER (O.S.)
     Is she okay?

Maurice looks up to see the driver of the Firebird walking towards him. He looks dazed.

Maurice doesn't waste another second and plunges his arm in the snow... deeper than before. His cheek pressed against the snow, almost laying flat on the ground.

Walk of Remembrance- Trilogy Part 1

>   MAURICE
>   (frantic)
>   Oh no... she's wearing a
> seat-belt.

Maurice fishes around... his teeth clenched... He lets out a POWERFUL GRUNT as he pulls back with all his strength -- a woman's WRIST appears first, then the tangled hair and then the body spills out onto the road next to Maurice.

The driver appears over the Woman and Maurice and loses it when he sees them.

>   DRIVER
>   It wasn't my fault. It
> wasn't my
>   fault.

Maurice, out of breath, clears the woman's face and mouth -- no movement. No sound.

>   MAURICE
>   Come on... please...

Maurice holds her nose and breaths into her mouth...

>   MAURICE
>   Please...

She doesn't respond.

CUT TO:

A FRIGHTENING FLASH

The mother's UNCONSCIOUS face turns into ELLEN. Her lifeless eyes -- her bruised cheek and forehead. Her neck at an awkward angle. Maurice stares down at his wife in horror.

      MAURICE
   No Ellen... don't die...

CUT TO:

THE MOTHER

being revived by Maurice. He pushes her chest in counting... push, count, breath... push, count, breath...

The mother's BODY TWITCHES, slightly at first -- then obviously... The mother let's out a FEW PAINFUL COUGHS.

She takes a breath. Life quickly returns to her body.

Walk of Remembrance- Trilogy Part 1

Maurice places her head in his lap and hugs her, lightly rocking back and forth. The tears streaming down his red face.

                  MAURICE
*Everything's going to be fine
Ellen. I won't let anything happen
to you. I love you sweetie.
Everything's going to be different
now.*

The SCENE BACKS OUT as Maurice comforts this stranger in his arms.

CUT TO:

EXT. ROAD - AFTERNOON

The police have descended on the scene. Traffic has been blocked off in both directions. The LIGHT thrown by the ambulances tints the snow and fields a THROBBING RED.

Maurice's face can be seen in the shadows of the backseat of a police car.

Walk of Remembrance- Trilogy Part 1

OUTSIDE THE CAR

OFFICER HANSEN AND OFFICER TANDY converse.

                    HANSEN
     What's his story?

                    TANDY
     His name is Maurice. He's dancing
     around everything else.

                    HANSEN
     Red flag, man.

                    TANDY
     If he's in trouble with the law --
     fine. Not our problem. He yanked
     two people from a car wreck, let's
     give him some space.

Hansen looks in at the drawn, exhausted face of Maurice through the window. Hansen opens the back door.

                    HANSEN
     Maurice, you need anything? Which
     way were you headed? We can drive

you.

                    MAURICE
No thank you officer. I'll walk.

Hansen throws a sharp glance to Tandy. Hansen turns back to Maurice.

                    HANSEN
Grub? Food? How about food? Our dime at the local diner...

Maurice mulls this offer.

                    HANSEN
Come on man, you're a hero. In Nebraska we don't let hero's walk around with empty stomachs.

Beat.

                    MAURICE
... I need to be brought back here.

                    HANSEN
Deal.

Walk of Remembrance- Trilogy Part 1

CUT TO:

INT. DINER - EVENING

The end of the meal. Maurice sits in a booth across from Hansen and Tandy. They watch as Maurice coughs violently into his napkin.

          HANSEN
    You look like shit Maurice.

Maurice takes a couple strained breaths.

          MAURICE
    Getting old.

          TANDY
    How long have you been footing it
    Maurice?

Beat.

          MAURICE
    Too long...
      (looks around)
    Excuse me gentlemen.

Maurice gets up and heads to the bathroom. Hansen and Tandy

stare at Maurice's shoulder bag laying on his seat.

                    HANSEN
          Red flags man.

                    TANDY
          Not our problem.

                    HANSEN
          Why so vague? Why so
          evasive? He
          could be somebody hot.

                    TANDY
          Not our problem.

                    HANSEN
          It's going to look
          beautiful when
          he turns out to be that
          animal who
          paid a visit to the
          Steadman's
          house.

                    TANDY
          This guy's not a
          murderer.

                    HANSEN
          If he is, half the town
          has seen us
          take him out for dinner
          like a
          couple of jack-asses.

That makes Tandy think.

      HANSEN
   If he's clean, he'll never know
    about it.

Tandy looks to the men's bathroom door.

      TANDY
   Do it quick.

Hansen instantly reaches over and begins rummaging through the shoulder bag. Hansen pulls out a little folder. He opens the folder to reveal an old certificate. Hansen shows Tandy the worn piece of paper.

      HANSEN
   A marriage certificate? Who the
    hell carries their marriage
    certificate around?

      TANDY
   Maurice and Ellen Parker... it was
    issued in Philly... Mr. Maurice
    Parker has come a long way from

Walk of Remembrance- Trilogy Part 1

              home. Why?

Hansen returns the certificate and folder to the bag and leaves the booth quickly.

CUT TO:

LATER

Maurice returns to the table to find only Tandy seated. Maurice sees Hansen in the phone booth at the far end of the diner.

                      TANDY
     Hansen's whipped. Has to call his
     wife every two hours or she'll go
     ballistic when he gets home.

CUT TO:

PHONE BOOTH

                      HANSEN
     P-A-R-K-E-R. Right. Get on the
     horn with Philly. Call me here.

Walk of Remembrance- Trilogy Part 1

CUT TO:

INT. PHILADELPHIA POLICE STATION - EVENING

Sergeant Dally packs his things to leave. He sees the light on LINE 1 LIGHT UP on his phone. He ignores it. The clerk sticks her head around the corner.

              CLERK
       Line one Sarg.

              DALLY
       I'm not here.

Dally zips his coat.

              CLERK
       It's the Nebraska state police.

              DALLY
       Nebraska?

              CLERK
       You know somebody named -
- Maurice
       Parker?

Dally freezes. He shakes his head as he unzips his jacket.

              DALLY

                    (smiles)
           That son of a bitch made it to
           Nebraska.

Dally grabs the phone.

CUT TO:

INT. GAZETTE BUILDING - EVENING

The C.B. CRACKLES WITH THE VOICE OF SERGEANT DALLY AND THE NEBRASKA POLICE.

MICHELLE, a very introverted intern, stares at the radio astonished.

CUT TO:

A SMALL SIDE OFFICE

It now has "KRIS REDDY" etched on it's door. Kris looks up from his desk at Michelle who stands in the doorway bright red.

                    KRIS
           What is it?

Michelle just points down the hall.

Walk of Remembrance- Trilogy Part 1

CUT TO:

OFFICE

Michelle scribbles down notes.

                        C.B./NEBRASKA POLICE
    ...He saved a little girl, and her mother. Pulled them right out of the car...

Kris stands, jaw hanging wide open.

                    KRIS
    Where is he?

Michelle checks her notes.

                  MICHELLE
        (very soft voice)
    Umm, Elm Creek, Nebraska.

Kris practically falls over. Michelle scribbles down more quotes.

                  MICHELLE
    This story is big huh?

                  KRIS
    Mammoth.

Walk of Remembrance- Trilogy Part 1

                MICHELLE
        The Gazette's small huh?

Beat.

                KRIS
        What are you saying? This story is
            too big for this paper?

                MICHELLE
           (flustered again)
        Umm, no. It's just that
--

                KRIS
        God damn, you're right... You don't
            say much Michelle, but what you say
            is golden.

Kris' mind is racing as the C.B. conversation continues.

CUT TO:

INT. DINER - NIGHT

Hansen scoffs down his third dessert. Maurice stares at him oddly.

The PAY PHONE RINGS. Hansen jumps to his feet too quickly.

Walk of Remembrance- Trilogy Part 1

He tries to recover.

                    HANSEN
                (too excited)
    I was expecting a call.

Hansen moves to the phone.

Tandy winks at Maurice with a smile.

                    TANDY
    Whipped.

CUT TO:

PHONE BOOTH

Hansen listens carefully to the officer on the line.

                 OFFICER (ON PHONE)
    ... I'm on first name basis with
    half the city of Philadelphia...
    Hansen, apparently this guy Parker
    lost his wife and went a little
    fruity. I spoke with his niece,
    Adelle Matlin and she says to

Walk of Remembrance- Trilogy Part 1

>   restrain him. That he's
> dangerous
>   to himself. She says to
> call when
>   we have him in the
> station.

>   HANSEN
>   Good work.

CUT TO:

EXT. POLICE CAR - NIGHT

The ride progresses in silence.
Hansen and Tandy in the
front seat. Maurice's head is
pressed against the back-seat
window. His eyes begin to shut
slightly as sleep overcomes
him. The car goes over a BUMP.
Maurice jars awake. He
glances out the window to see a
highway sign swish by in the
HEADLIGHTS. 'ROUTE 80 EAST'.

East? Maurice looks around quickly
at the passing scenery.

>   MAURICE
>   Where are you taking me?

Hansen and Tandy exchange looks.

>   HANSEN

Walk of Remembrance - Trilogy Part 1

> I'm going to drop off Tandy at the station and then drop you back.

TANDY
That's all right isn't it?

MAURICE
Sure.

Hansen looks back to the road. The drive continues in silence. Tandy checks his watch just when a CLICK -- A HARD WIND -- AND A METALLIC SLAM in quick succession shakes the car.

HANSEN
What the hell was that?

Tandy looks back -- Maurice is GONE. The back seat empty. Tandy stares out the blackness of the back window.

TANDY
Shit! He jumped!

HANSEN
Jumped where?

TANDY

Walk of Remembrance- Trilogy Part 1

          Out of the car. He jumped out of the god damn car!

CUT TO:

EXT. FOREST - NIGHT

Maurice staggers through the naked trees. Thin trees every few feet with no branches. The snow ankle deep.

Maurice braces himself against a trunk, checking his hands. His vision blurs as he stares down at his scraped bloody palms.

The forest clears quickly into an open field. Far in the distance across the field of white is a small pointed building standing alone. The glow of a LIGHT can be seen through the windows.

Maurice trudges through the deeper snow. Stumbling many times. The frigid wind pushing him to his knees. Maurice keeps moving -- the field seems endless...

Walk of Remembrance- Trilogy Part 1

CUT TO:

DRIVEWAY

Maurice's feet hit the snow of the driveway, just as his legs buckle -- his face HITS the snow hard. He manages to roll over on his back with great effort. He stares up at the pointed building -- the dull light becoming duller... something blocks the light. A man. Maurice feels himself rise into the air as two powerful arms scoop him off the ice.

A PRIEST carries him into the doors of a CHURCH.

CUT TO:

INT. BACK ROOM OF CHURCH - NIGHT

A dimly lit cathedral. Six foot six, FATHER BERCHMAN walks down the center isle of the cathedral, through a cloth curtain and into a

BACK ROOM

where Maurice is sitting in a chair wrapped in a blanket.

Walk of Remembrance- Trilogy Part 1

                MAURICE
       What did they ask?

                FATHER
       If I had seen you. By the way I'm
       sorry about your wife. They told
       me.

                MAURICE
       Thank you... I'm sorry you had to
       lie. It must have been difficult.

                FATHER
       I asked the officers if you had
       committed some crime... If they had
       said 'yes', you would be speaking
       with them right now.

This is the father's own room. Very sparse as one would expect. He moves to his bureau and retrieves some pills.

                FATHER
       Take these, and if you're up to it,
       try to explain how it is you came

Walk of Remembrance- Trilogy Part 1

></p>
    to be sitting here.

Maurice follows the father's instructions and tightens the blanket around his shoulders.

      MAURICE
  I'm walking for my wife.

Beat.

      FATHER
  To where?

      MAURICE
  Pacifica, California.

      FATHER
  From where?

      MAURICE
  Philadelphia, Pennsylvania.

      FATHER
  I see.

Beat. The father nods as if this is not shocking news.

      FATHER
  Why?

      MAURICE
  Do you believe a person's soul

Walk of Remembrance- Trilogy Part 1

　　　　　lives on after their death?

　　　　　　　　FATHER
　　　　Most certainly.

　　　　　　　　MAURICE
　　　　And that that soul takes part of
　　　　the person they were on this earth
　　　　with them.

　　　　　　　　FATHER
　　　　That's a reasonable assumption.

　　　　　　　　MAURICE
　　　　I don't want my wife's soul having
　　　　any doubts.

　　　　　　　　FATHER
　　　　Doubts? About what?

　　　　　　　　MAURICE
　　　　About my love for her.

The father nods with understanding as if everything became
very clear with that statement.

　　　　　　　　FATHER
　　　　You don't have to prove anything to
　　　　her.

Walk of Remembrance- Trilogy Part 1

                    MAURICE
          I'm not proving to her.
I'm
          showing her. And I know
I don't
          have to. I want to.
I've
          realized, love is about
giving.
          I'm alive, I can still
give to her.
          I want to give her
everything I
          can.

The father studies this stranger
before him with great
admiration.

                    MAURICE
          There are some people,
including
          those officers, that are
trying to
          stop me. They mean well.
But they
          don't understand. I
wouldn't
          either if I were them.

Maurice struggles with the last
words. He slumps back --
physically drained.

Walk of Remembrance- Trilogy Part 1

The father gets up and takes the empty glass of water from Maurice's hands.

                  FATHER
    I want you to stay here a few days
        until you're better. You're no use
        to your wife in this condition.

The father moves for the curtain.

                  MAURICE
    You think I'm crazy too.

The father turns and smiles warmly.

                  FATHER
    I have spent my life dedicated to
        love. Love of God. Love of
        humanity. And here you are living
        through love. Bathing in it.
        Using its strength, its magic, its
        ability to overcome any barrier...
        If you are crazy, I hope my
        insanity is not far off.

Walk of Remembrance- Trilogy Part 1

Maurice's eyes well up instantly.

CUT TO:

EXT. CHURCH - WESTERN HIGHWAY - DAY

Father Berchman wraps one powerful hand around a tiny silver cross dangling from his neck. The other hand waves high into the air at the shrinking figure of Maurice Parker walking through the snow.

DISSOLVE TO:

HIGHWAY

The long trek continues. The black tar of the roads peek out in spots as the SUN BEATS down on the flatlands. Maurice drapes his worn scarf around a melting snowman.

DISSOLVE TO:

RESTAURANT

We are looking inside a fancy Center-City Philadelphia

Walk of Remembrance- Trilogy Part 1

restaurant. Adelle and Gerald are seated by an enormous bay window. A waiter comes to their table with their main course. Gerald watches the food being served with great anticipation.

Gerald's eyes drift out the window to the magazine stand on the sidewalk... He squints to see better. Realization hits hard... His eyes light up. He looks to Adelle and back to the magazine stand.

In a mad race for time, Gerald begins to devour the food on his plate. The waiter and Adelle watch him in shock. Adelle glances out the window. Her eyes squint... then light up. She jumps to her feet and grabs Gerald by the arm, a fork full of food drops to his plate. Gerald looks back at his full plate longingly as Adelle pulls him out of the restaurant.

The waiter looks out the window to the magazine stand. He squints.

CUT TO:

MAGAZINE STAND

The NEW YORK TIMES are hung like stockings around the border of the stand. On the front pages, a singular headline stands out among the others:

"A JOURNEY OF THE HEART"

A large PHOTO OF MAURICE is next to the headline.

DISSOLVE TO:

DINER

A red-headed waitress slices a credit card through the machine and waits... Green computer letters blink - "This account has been closed."

The waitress returns with the card -- she shakes her head "No" at Maurice who digs into his wallet for cash.

DISSOLVE TO:

MOTEL

Walk of Remembrance- Trilogy Part 1

Maurice slides two twenties across the counter to the motel manager. Maurice checks the remaining bills in his wallet... only a few bills left.

In the motel room we find Maurice sitting over the edge of a bed buckled over in a coughing attack. It finally stops. Maurice flops back to the pillows, completely drained.

DISSOLVE TO:

ROADS

The flatlands have vanished. The roads now serpentine through mountain ranges.

VIEW FROM THE MOUNTAIN RANGE; Maurice moves like a grain of dust over the black line of the road.

Maurice rests every half mile. He labors up every incline with ultimate effort. He braces himself with a branch serving as a make due crutch.

Maurice spots a small town nestled in the arms of the

Walk of Remembrance- Trilogy Part 1

mountain range. He begins the
journey to rest.

DISSOLVE TO:

GROCERIES

Maurice pays for his food with the
last few bills in his
wallet.

DISSOLVE TO:

ROAD

Another stick serves as a walking
cane. The multi layers of
clothes have been shed for a short-
sleeve shirt. Maurice
follows a dirt road that breaks
free of the mountains and
into the open country again.

SUPERIMPOSE: COALVILLE, UTAH...
MILE 2,472

CUT TO:

EXT. DRIVEWAY - DUSK

A dust covered mailbox at the end
of a long dirt driveway.

Walk of Remembrance- Trilogy Part 1

Maurice wipes the mailbox clean with his hand. The name emerges like an ancient inscription from beneath the mud... "CALDWELLS."

CUT TO:

FRONT DOOR

Maurice tentatively moving to the front door. His hand instinctively clutches his empty stomach.

The wind blows gently. Maurice shuts his eyes and takes a deep breath. He opens his eyes slowly to see a dinner table being set. Potatoes, gravy, fresh baked bread... floating through the half open window to Maurice's thankful smile.
THE SOUNDS OF CHILDREN AND ADULTS CAN BE HEARD INSIDE.

The first LIGHT KNOCKS go unheard with all the commotion.
HARDER. The door squeaks open. Maurice puts on his best smile... the door opens wider -- no one stands before him.

     BOY (O.S.)
 Hi.

Walk of Remembrance- Trilogy Part 1

Maurice looks down to find an adorable little boy, black hair, big eyes and an even bigger grin. This is three year old ISAAC CALDWELL.

> MAURICE
> Well, hello.

> ISAAC
> I'm Isaac... I'm three.

> MAURICE
> I'm Maurice Parker... I'm much older than three. Are your parents home?

Beat. Isaac thinks.

> ISAAC
> You know what, I can play baseball with my brothers when I'm bigger.

> MAURICE
> Is that right?

> ISAAC
> You know what... I'm just little now, but I'll be big soon.

Walk of Remembrance- Trilogy Part 1

                    MAURICE
          You'll probably be bigger
than your
          brothers.

                    ISAAC
          Yeah!

Isaac is happy with this thought.

Maurice looks up as MRS. CALDWELL
comes to the door.

                    MRS. CALDWELL
          Who are you talking to
Isaac?

Mrs. Caldwell stops as she stares
at Maurice.

                    MAURICE
          Hello, I'm Maurice
Parker. I'm
          just passing through and
I need to
          conserve what little
funds I
          have... I need some food
and a roof
          to sleep under for one
night... Now
          I don't look like much,
but if
          there are any things that
need to

>   get done around the house
--

Mrs. Caldwell doesn't listen, but instead yells behind the door.

>   MRS. CALDWELL
>   Dave... you're not going
to believe
>   who's here.

Maurice looks at her oddly. MR. CALDWELL comes to the door; his face lights up.

>   MRS. CALDWELL
>   This is Maurice Parker --
the one
>   walking for his wife.

Mr. Caldwell is completely floored. So, for that matter is Maurice. Mr. Caldwell puts out his hand with awe.

>   MR. CALDWELL
>   If that ain't fate?...
Hi, I'm Dave
>   Caldwell. I do the copy
for the
>   anchor on the evening
news down
>   here.

>   MAURICE

Walk of Remembrance- Trilogy Part 1

>   *Evening News?*
>
>   MR. CALDWELL
>   *We did a piece after your story ran*
>   *in the New York Times.*

Maurice is truly surprised.

>   MAURICE
>   *New York Times?*

Mrs. Caldwell ushers Maurice in the doorway by the elbow.

>   MRS. CALDWELL
>   *Someone said they spotted you in*
>   *town... Mr. Parker, you're a*
>   *celebrity.*

CUT TO:

INT. CALDWELL KITCHEN - NIGHT

The Caldwell family dinner... all twelve of them. Ten children talk and reach for food. Maurice sits at the end talking, enjoying and sharing. Isaac sits next to him proudly. Maurice has blended in as another member of this family.

CUT TO:

INT. CALDWELL GUEST BEDROOM - NIGHT

An inviting room. The kind prepared for visiting grandmothers and grandfathers to stay in.

Maurice checks himself out in the mirror... his borrowed pajamas fit nicely.

He moves to the window and stares at the moon lit landscape... enormous, endless, dwarfing.

The rocking chair CREAKS as Maurice melts into it. He rubs his calves slowly, the pain evident in his face. His head leans back after a moment... on the verge of sleep.

The SOUND OF TINY FOOTSTEPS stirs him. He looks to the doorway to find Isaac standing quietly at the door in his baseball P.J.s.

                    MAURICE

Walk of Remembrance- Trilogy Part 1

        I thought you were asleep.

                ISAAC
        You know what... I remembered you
          were here and I woke up.

Isaac walks silently to Maurice... Tip-toeing all the way.

                MAURICE
        Your parents would want you to be
          in bed.

                ISAAC
        You tell stories?

                MAURICE
        Oh no... I'm not good at that.
        Very bad in fact...

Too late. Isaac climbs up into Maurice's lap with great effort. Maurice looks down at Isaac who waits patiently for him to begin.

                MAURICE
        I would be exceedingly boring.

Isaac waits.

Walk of Remembrance- Trilogy Part 1

                    MAURICE
          I don't do these type of
things.

Isaac -- still waiting.

                    MAURICE
          See there are two kinds
of people
               in this world.
                    (beat)
          ... Just a short one
okay?

Isaac gets in position, cradled in
Maurice's arms. Maurice
searches for something to say.

                    MAURICE
          There was a boy named
Isaac who
               wanted to play baseball,
but he was
               too small and no one
would let him
               play... but he kept
practicing by
               himself -- waiting... He
went to
               every game and sat in the
stands
               with his glove.

                    ISAAC
          You know what... maybe I
ran onto

Walk of Remembrance- Trilogy Part 1

>   the field and hit a home run.
>
>   MAURICE
>   Who's telling this story?
>
> Isaac points to Maurice.
>
>   MAURICE
>   Good, now the team had this great
>   big player -- Big Billy. He was
>   the best. He had them in the World
>   Super-Bowl-Championship of little
>   kids baseball. But right before
>   the game, the second best player on
>   the team was suspended because he
>   played a prank on a nice man who
>   owned a book store... When that boy
>   grew up he was convicted on
>   burglary charges and spent fifteen
>   years in prison -- where he
>   belongs.

Isaac didn't understand that last part.

                  MAURICE
    Anyway, Big Billy needed another
        player so he yelled into the
        stands. 'Who can play baseball?'
        And there was a little voice that
        yelled out, 'Me, I can play.'
        Everyone turned to see a little boy
        standing with a glove.

                  ISAAC
            (beaming)
    That's me.

                  MAURICE
    Right. But everyone saw how small
        Isaac was and laughed... but not
        Big Billy. He stared at Isaac
        carefully and then told him to join
        the game. It came to the end of
        the game. It was the eleventh or

> *twelfth inning or whatever is the last inning of a game...*

>>> ISAAC
> *Nine.*

>>> MAURICE
> *Okay nine. Big Billy's team was losing and he was on base. That's when Isaac came up. He could barely hold the bat... Big Billy winked at Isaac... The ball was pitched -- Isaac hit the ball hard. It soared up and out over the stadium. Everyone cheered. Isaac hit a home run and won the game. After the game, Isaac asked Big Billy why he let he play. Big Billy smiled and said, I wasn't always Big Billy, I was Little Billy first... Isaac and Big Billy*

                    went off after the game
and read a
                    classic book together.
The end.

                         ISAAC
                    You know what -- that was
a really
                    good story... Tell it
again.

Maurice has to smile as Isaac looks
up anxiously.

                         MAURICE
                    There was a boy named
Isaac who
                    liked to play baseball...

WE BACK OUT as Maurice rocks back
and forth in his chair.
Isaac falling asleep in his arms.

CUT TO:

EXT. CALDWELL DRIVEWAY - MORNING

The family dog "Max", scurries up
and down with great
excitement. Max can sense
something big is happening.

The Caldwell clan, one and all has
gathered at the end of

Walk of Remembrance- Trilogy Part 1

their driveway. Maurice is
escorted out by Isaac who clings
tightly to his hand. Mr. Caldwell
meets Maurice halfway and
pulls him aside.

                    MR. CALDWELL
          That's a nice watch.

Maurice looks down at his beat-up
Seiko.

                    MR. CALDWELL
          I've always wanted a
watch like
          that.

                    MAURICE
             (unstrapping it)
          It's yours.

                    MR. CALDWELL
          No. I won't take it
unless I pay
          for it... Let's see,
that's a
          pretty nice watch -- I
can see
          that.

Maurice watches him suspiciously as
he pulls out an envelope
from his jacket pocket.

                    MR. CALDWELL

Walk of Remembrance- Trilogy Part 1

>   Let's say I give you what's in this
>   envelope for that beautiful watch.

Maurice is handed the envelope. He opens it to find a thick
PILE OF CASH, TENS AND TWENTIES.

>   MR. CALDWELL
>   I really want that watch.

>   MAURICE
>   This isn't right.

>   MR. CALDWELL
>   This is my only chance to get a
>   watch like that. It would mean a
>   lot to me and my family. Please
>   take it. It really isn't that
>   much.

Maurice stares into the envelope emotionally and hands over
the watch tentatively.

>   MAURICE
>   This is a loan.

Mr. Caldwell straps on the watch and then hugs Maurice.

Walk of Remembrance- Trilogy Part 1

The rest of the family say their good-byes.

Isaac won't let go of Maurice's hand as he walks out into the street.

                    MR. CALDWELL
            Isaac, come back here.

Isaac just holds on tighter. After Maurice and Isaac have walked a few steps out into the street, Maurice kneels down.

                    MAURICE
            I have to go now.

Isaac's bottom lip protrudes as he tries not to cry. Maurice has to hold back a few tears himself. He hugs Isaac tightly.

                    MAURICE
                (whispers)
            Why didn't I meet you fifteen years
                ago?

Maurice pulls away from Isaac slowly. Isaac runs to his mother's arms. Maurice waves good-bye to the Caldwells as he heads down the road.

Walk of Remembrance- Trilogy Part 1

CUT TO:

EXT. ROAD - DAY

Maurice stops, bends down to the road and picks up a TORN WHITE PAPER STREAMER that spiraled its way to his feet.

He looks ahead and finds both sides of the street lined with parked cars. Some of the cars are decorated with white streamers.

CUT TO:

OUTDOOR WEDDING

A beautiful canopy of flowers sits at the end of ten rows of lawn chairs. Maurice watches from near the cars. He smiles as the young bride and groom nervously say their vows. Everyone LAUGHS warmly as the groom stumbles over his lines.

CUT TO:

INT. CHAPEL - DAY (FLASHBACK)

Walk of Remembrance- Trilogy Part 1

Moments before the ceremony. The guests are seated. The ORGAN is PLAYING.

CUT TO:

SIDE ROOM

Young Maurice sits on a chair in a tuxedo staring out the half-open door to an OLD MAN who tries to gain his balance by holding onto the wall. Maurice is upset. He runs his fingers through his hair.

THE DOOR OPENS wide as Young Ellen comes in. She is wearing her WEDDING GOWN. White lace, tight at the arms and waist -- she looks stunning.

      ELLEN
  What's wrong? They said something
    was wrong?

Maurice stares at his rented shoes.

      MAURICE
  I'm fine.

Ellen moves to him and kneels before him. She lifts his chin.

> ELLEN
> Everyone's here. Everything. looks beautiful. They even got the white dove I wanted for the cake -- so what's wrong? What is it?

Maurice moves his gaze from her to the half open door.

> MAURICE
> It's him.

Ellen looks back.

> ELLEN
> Your father?

> MAURICE
> He's plastered.

> ELLEN
> That's okay -- really it is.

> MAURICE
> No it's not. He should be here with me now, not trying to find some fucking bottle of Johnny

Walker. He's never been there for
me. I've always been alone.

Maurice looks like he may cry.

      MAURICE
I'm afraid Ellen... I'm scared of
being alone again. What if one day
you realize how boring I am? What
if one day you realize you're not
happy?
   (beat)
I could have been alone before, but
now you've changed things. I can't
be alone anymore Ellen. I'm scared
what's going to happen to me.

Ellen takes both his hands and squeezes them between hers.

      ELLEN
The day I met you, I gave you my
heart. Today, I give you my soul.

Walk of Remembrance- Trilogy Part 1

          Where ever you are, where ever you
          go, I will be with you. Maurice
          Parker, I promise --
             (she shakes him with
             emphasis)
          I promise, you will never be alone
          again.

CUT TO:

EXT. OUTDOOR MARRIAGE - DAY (PRESENT)

The bride and groom run through a shower of rice into their limousine.

CUT TO:

INSIDE LIMOUSINE

They wave through the window as the car pulls away. They settle in and look to the seat across from them. On the seat is a fresh flower. Next to the flower is a note. The groom picks it up and shows it to the bride. It reads:

Walk of Remembrance- Trilogy Part 1

                    "CHERISH EVERYDAY
TOGETHER"

It is signed "M.P."

The bride and groom look at each other curiously.

CUT TO:

ROAD

The limousine passes Maurice on the road as he walks.

CUT TO:

INT. GAZETTE BUILDING - DAY

A fax machine rolls out a tongue of information. Michelle, the intern, snatches it and jogs through the maze of desks.

CUT TO:

KRIS'S OFFICE

Michelle catches the tail end of a telephone conversation.

                    KRIS

> -- Come on Pete, this is important,
> this is racism in our backyard...
> Aw, that's bull... just think about
> it, okay?

Kris hangs up.

                      KRIS
> They're pushing my Jewish temple
> vandalism story to the Metro
> section...

Kris notices Michelle's familiar bright red face.

                      KRIS
> What?

Michelle is completely flustered as usual.

                      KRIS
> Michelle, breathe... that's it,
> what is it, talk to me.

                      MICHELLE
>   (hands the fax over)
> Umm, Coalville Utah.

Walk of Remembrance- Trilogy Part 1

Kris studies the fax before jumping up from his desk and moving to the wall. An enormous U.S. MAP covers three quarters of the wall. RED TACKS mark a trail across the United States, beginning with Philadelphia. Kris puts a red tack at the top right corner of Utah.

Kris notices through the open officer door that Frank and Seth are listening in. Kris nods to Michelle. Who immediately shuts the door on their view. Kris waves bye before it closes.

      KRIS
  He's taking highway 80 all the way.

Kris paces the room -- charged with excitement -- eyes occasionally stopping on the map. Michelle watches Kris' animated expressions.

      KRIS
  You know what this is, don't you?
    It's a miracle. Not like... 'It
    was a miracle little Johnny passed

Walk of Remembrance- Trilogy Part 1

>   his math test.' No!
This is a
            real miracle... Turning
water to
            wine kind of miracle.
People
            should know about this,
everyone,
            every single person...
It's time
            for a blitz. Let's see
what kind
            of TV interest we can
generate.

Michelle enjoys watching Kris when he's like this.

>   MICHELLE
>   Umm, he's going to make
it isn't
>   he?

>   KRIS
>   Maybe.

Kris studies the map.

>   KRIS
>   But he hasn't hit the
toughest
>   miles yet.

CUT TO:

Walk of Remembrance- Trilogy Part 1

INT. ADELLE'S LIVING ROOM - NIGHT

The lights are out. The FLICKER FROM THE TV dances over Adelle and Gerald. Adelle is fast asleep. Gerald is having a late night sandwich. NIGHTLINE comes on the TV.

                TV ANCHOR
    What would you do for love? This
    is the question Americans are
    starting to ask themselves. The
    incredible tale of Maurice Parker's
    walk across the country has caught
    the imaginations of young and old.

Gerald sighs. He puts the sandwich on the plate and hands it to his left -- obediently. PAN TO LEFT to find Adelle wide awake now. She glares at the TV screen silently as she takes the sandwich and dumps it in the waste basket releasing some of her frustration.

A COMPUTER MAP OF THE U.S. trails Maurice's walk on the screen.

Walk of Remembrance- Trilogy Part 1

> TV ANCHOR
> At 44, this bookstore owner from Wynnewood Pennsylvania has tallied an estimated 2,400 miles. His latest appearance in Coalville Utah brought the spotlight of the country to that small town.

> GERALD
> Coalville Utah?

> ADELLE
> I can't believe it.

> TV ANCHOR
> Whatever has carried Mr. Parker through snow and rain and thousands of miles of this countryside, will have to carry him through the most dangerous part of his trek... The three hundred miles through the sweltering roads of Nevada...

Walk of Remembrance- Trilogy Part 1

                  ADELLE
        My God.

CUT TO:

EXT. HIGHWAY - DAY

A merciless sun beats down on a long stretch of highway. The black tar from the road melting slightly.

No sign of Maurice. WE SEE into the distance, not a soul in sight. WE LOOK to a hillside a hundred meters from the road. There we see a figure lying still in the shade of an overhanging rock formation.

Maurice has a towel over his eyes and his feet propped up on his shoulder bag. He is fast asleep.

DISSOLVE TO:

DUSK

The SUN TURNS RED for one brilliant moment before hiding behind the horizon. Like an alarm went off, Maurice wakes up

Walk of Remembrance- Trilogy Part 1

and packs his things.

CUT TO:

ROAD

The MOONLIGHT outlines a line figure hobbling his way step by step with a walking stick.

The air fills with a POWERFUL RUMBLE. Maurice turns to see a wave of rocks and sand slide down a hillside to the road.
They CAUSE A GREAT THUNDER that settles to dust. Maurice walks down the center of the highway away from the hillside.

DISSOLVE TO:

EXT. HIGHWAY - DAWN

THE FIERY NEVADA SUN BEGINS ITS ASCENT INTO THE SKY. Maurice looks bad. He's breathing heavy as he moves up a steep incline by the side of the road. His feet slide on the loose dirt. Maurice looks like he could collapse at any moment.

He makes it to the indentation in the hillside -- just enough

Walk of Remembrance- Trilogy Part 1

room to lay down in the shade.
Maurice lays out slowly. He
pries off his sneakers, band-aids
and blisters cover every
inch of his feet. Maurice dumps
the sand out of his sneakers
and painfully pulls them back on.
His eyes close as he tries
to unbutton his jacket... too late
he's asleep.

Maurice's bed is a rock that juts
from the side of the
hill... First WE SEE nothing, then
some grains of sand escape
from the crack where the rock meets
the hillside. The CRACK
BECOMES SLIGHTLY LARGER -- PULLING
AWAY FROM THE HILL BY A
FRACTION OF AN INCH. It stabilizes
there.

Maurice unaware of his precarious
situation sleeps twenty
five feet above the ground.

CUT TO:

MID-DAY

Another sizzler. Temperatures in
the nineties. The sun is
directly overhead.

Walk of Remembrance- Trilogy Part 1

Maurice stirs in his sleep, moving closer to the edge of the rock.

A STEADY STREAM OF SAND POURS FROM THE CRACK...
A SLIGHT TREMOR...
THEN THE FRIGHTENING SOUND OF ROCK MOVING AGAINST ROCK...

Maurice wakes up as he begins to slide off... Hands scraping at the dirt... He SLIDES OFF THE ROCK... Feet and hands desperately trying to cling to the hillside... He picks up speed as he tumbles down... Maurice looks down in time to see a small jut in the rock hurtling towards him... no time for panic... SLAM! A SICKENING CRACK OF BONE as Maurice HITS the rock square in the ribs... Maurice flops down the rest of the slope like a rag doll... he comes to rest in the dirt, clutching his ribs. The sun beats down on his stunned eyes.

Maurice stares up at the dizzying slope. Sand still trickling down to a stop. He doesn't try to move for the first few seconds. His breathing increasingly erratic.

Walk of Remembrance- Trilogy Part 1

Maurice drags himself to sit upright. The sharp pains causing a distorted grimace on his face. A short rest, before working his way to his feet.

CUT TO:

HIGHWAY

Maurice uses a highway guardrail as a backrest. He takes a seat in the dirt. Maurice's hair is damp with sweat. His breathing relegated to slow gasps. His left hand covering his rib cage protectively. Blood begins to trickle through the spaces between his fingers.

Maurice closes his eyes for a moment, before his bent leg goes into spasms... Maurice is forced to straighten the leg instantly... jarring his tender rib cafe... Maurice clings to the back of his thigh... Maurice is defeated... On the verge of tears.

He glances way down the road and spots a TINY CLOUD OF SMOKE miles away in the distance. A car is moving in his direction.

Walk of Remembrance- Trilogy Part 1

Maurice looks up into the DAZZLING WHITE SKY. Drops of sweat falling into his eyes.

              MAURICE
        (whisper)
    It's over Ellen... I failed you
        again.

Maurice looks down the road at the cloud of dust growing larger.

              MAURICE
    I tried Ellen, I really tried... I
        don't have the strength.

The cloud is now clearly a car... Maurice stares up into the sky again... The tears racing the sweat down his cheeks. Maurice YELLS TO THE HEAVENS.

              MAURICE
    You said I would never be alone!...
        You promised...
           (his yelling turns to
           sobs)
    ... You promised.

Maurice's is interrupted by A SLIGHT RUSTLING BEHIND HIS

Walk of Remembrance- Trilogy Part 1

HEAD. Maurice turns and looks through his tears...

There, a few feet from him, perched quietly and majestically on the guardrail is a GOLDEN EAGLE. It stands two and half feet tall. It spreads it's great wings. The feathers expand like a blanket, spanning six feet, and throwing a gentle shade on Maurice's face.

Maurice is frozen in wonder. The MAGIC of the moment glows in his eyes. Maurice's face gains life... The dark feathered eagle stands like a god before Maurice. The moment is breathtaking.

CUT TO:

ROAD

The car on the road, takes the last quarter mile in seconds... SCREECHING IT'S BRAKES at the sight of Maurice on the side of the road.

Maurice turns away from the bird as the car pulls up. The driver gets out and calls over the hood.

Walk of Remembrance- Trilogy Part 1

>   DRIVER
>   Hey, man are you okay?

Maurice's face filled with strength. He grins through the pain.

>   MAURICE
>   I'm fine.

>   DRIVER
>   What the hell are you doing out
>   here? You need a ride somewhere?

>   MAURICE
>   No thank you.

The driver is concerned. He opens the driver door.

>   DRIVER
>   You by yourself?

Beat.

>   MAURICE
>   No.

This pacifies the driver somewhat. He nods and gets in the car. Maurice watches as the car pulls away.

Walk of Remembrance- Trilogy Part 1

*He turns back to the guardrail --
the eagle is gone. Maurice
looks up into the sky. The Golden
Eagle is flying
overhead... a tiny dot against the
blazing sun.*

*Maurice struggles to his feet using
the guardrail as support.
Maurice takes his first step...*

DISSOLVE TO:

EXT. SUBURBAN STREET - DAY

*Suburbia. Rows of similar houses
with small lawns and custom
mailboxes. Beautiful trees line
the streets creating a
canopy over the roadway.*

*Two women sit on a swing on the
front porch of a small
suburban home. JANIS AND AMMIE'S
conversation is cut in mid
sentence.*

     JANIS
 Who is that?

     AMMIE
 I don't know. What's the matter
 with him?

Walk of Remembrance- Trilogy Part 1

Janis and Ammie stare to the street where a sunburnt MAURICE staggers in a daze.

MAURICE'S POV

Maurice is on the edge of darkness... the trees and faces swimming -- mixed with the colors of red and blue cloth waving in the wind... Images come in and out of focus... two women walking towards him... Maurice clutches his head as the trees start to swim faster -- color, lights, houses...

DISSOLVING TO BLACK:

Maurice collapses in the middle of this suburban street.
Janis and Ammie run to his side.

SUPERIMPOSED: "ROSEVILLE, CALIFORNIA... MILE 3,205"

DISSOLVE TO:

INT. HOSPITAL ROOM - DAY

Maurice lays still on a hospital bed. His eyes slowly force themselves open.

Walk of Remembrance- Trilogy Part 1

> NURSE (O.S.)
> Good morning Mr. Parker.

Maurice turns his head to the side. A pretty woman in her late twenties, with LARGE LOCKS OF BROWN HAIR smiles back. This is STEPHANIE.

> STEPHANIE
> There are a lot of people worried about you.

> MAURICE
> (softly)
> Where am I?

> STEPHANIE
> In a hospital.

> MAURICE
> Which hospital? Did you take me back?

Stephanie understands his worry.

> STEPHANIE
> You are in St. Vincent's Hospital in Roseville California. You've been here three days.

Maurice closes his eyes in relief.

Walk of Remembrance- Trilogy Part 1

                    MAURICE
          Thank God.

CUT TO:

INT. HOSPITAL - AFTERNOON

The room is crowded. Maurice is now propped up in a seated position. He tries to digest a set of fish sticks on a tray.

                    MAURICE
          I can't believe you're
here. I'm
               touched.

Maurice looks across to ADELLE AND GERALD.

                    MAURICE
          Are you two planning
kids?

                    ADELLE
          Maybe later.

                    MAURICE
          You should definitely
have
               children. They're really
special.

Walk of Remembrance- Trilogy Part 1

*Adelle and Gerald are in shock.
Maurice forks another fish
stick with a smile.*

>   ADELLE
>   I don't think you realize how
>   serious this is Uncle.

>   MAURICE
>   How serious is it?

*DR. RAY, who has been standing by
the window listening, steps
forward.*

>   DR. RAY
>   You have two broken ribs, a
>   punctured spleen and Acute
>   Rheumatoid Arthritis.*

*Maurice gives a comforting smile to
Adelle.*

>   DR. RAY
>   The normal amount of build up in
>   your arteries has been aggravated
>   by over exertion. This is called,
>   "Claudication," As a result, there

>   isn't enough circulation
> to your
>   body. That accounts for
> the
>   discoloration in your
> extremities
>   and the muscle spasms I'm
> sure
>   you've encountered.
>
>   MAURICE
>   Can it kill me?
>
>   DR. RAY
>   It can, but it'll have to
> wait in
>   line.

This surprises Maurice.

>   DR. RAY
>   We ran a C.T. and an
> M.R.I. We
>   found bleeding in your
> brain. Your
>   collapse was caused by
> "Transient
>   Cerebral-Ischemia"... a
> sudden loss
>   of blood circulation to
> the brain.
>   In other words, Mr.
> Parker, you had
>   a mild stroke.

There is dead silence in the room.

                    MAURICE
                  (scared)
            I suppose I over did it.

Adelle moves over to Maurice's side and holds his hand.

                    MAURICE
            What steps do we take now?

                    DR. RAY
            We operate. We find the artery in
            the brain and close the bleeding...
            I just did this procedure on a
            Senator and he's doing fine.

                    MAURICE
            What are the odds? Do I have a
            fifty-fifty chance of surviving the
            operation?

                    DR. RAY
            It's hard to say. It's a delicate
            surgery. There's no getting around
            the fact that it's a very high-risk

Walk of Remembrance- Trilogy Part 1

situation.

Adelle strokes Maurice's hair. Maurice stares down at his food before looking up with great resolve.

                MAURICE
    Then it'll have to wait until I
    finish.

                ADELLE
    What?

                MAURICE
    I finish the walk, and then we may
    take all the chances we want.

The room is stunned. Adelle gets off the bed and collects herself.

                ADELLE
    Listen to me very carefully,
    because I don't want you to
    misunderstand me... The walk is
    over Uncle Maurice. Done.
    Finished. You've made it to

Walk of Remembrance- Trilogy Part 1

>California, it was a miracle, now
>let's try to save your life.

                MAURICE
         (louder)
>I'm completing the walk. I'm almost there.

                DR. RAY
>Okay, Maurice keep it calm...
        (beat)
>We can talk about this again, but just so you know, we have a guard on this floor who's sole job it is to keep an eye on you.

Maurice is crushed.

                DR. RAY
>There are a lot of people out there who would like to see you finish, including me, but I'm not willing to put your life in anymore risk than it is... We do the operation,

Walk of Remembrance - Trilogy Part 1

>   *and when you're better, you finish*
>   *the walk.*

The room is dead again. Maurice drowns in his thoughts.

CUT TO:

INT. HOSPITAL CHAPEL - AFTERNOON

A small chapel. Stain glass windows overlooking the parking lot. Maurice sits in his wheel chair at the back of the room. A few other patients are scattered in the four small pews.

Maurice has his hands folded tightly and stares up at the statue of Mary. His concentration is broken as a man in a full black suit and black shirt sits next to him. Maurice nods at the priest.

>   PRIEST
>   *Hello, Mr. Parker.*

>   MAURICE
>   *Hello.*

>   PRIEST
>   *How are you feeling?*

Walk of Remembrance- Trilogy Part 1

                    MAURICE
          Confused. I'm not sure
what to do
          now. I'm not sure what
he wants
          for me.

                    PRIEST
          He wants to reward you...
That's
          why I'm here.

                    MAURICE
               (a little confused)
          What do you mean?

                    PRIEST
          I mean you've done a
great thing.
          You should be rewarded
monetarily.

Maurice is lost.

                    PRIEST
          What's your shoe size?

                    MAURICE
          What? Who are you?

The priest reaches into his jacket
-- for the first time WE
SEE a Polo design on his shirt and
a gaudy gold chain around
his neck.

Walk of Remembrance- Trilogy Part 1

                    PRIEST
          Clive Silver -- Marketing
Executive
          at Reebok.

Maurice stares at the card in disbelief.

                    CLIVE
          We want you to do some
spots for
          us.

                    MAURICE
          What the hell is this?

Some of the patients turn around.

                    CLIVE
          I'm talking six figures,
pay or
          play -- for two spots.
We want to
          push a new line with
you...
          America's New Hero.

Maurice is flustered. He can't take this. His eyes become desperate.

Clive waves his hands in the air excitedly.

                    CLIVE

Walk of Remembrance- Trilogy Part 1

>Imagine grainy black and white shots of long stretches of highway -- quick cuts with a slow pounding beat underneath... Then we see a man walking up a steep incline -- it's you Maurice. We see shots of you walking. Cut. Cut. Cut. Fast... Music crescendoes -- Bham! Close up -- and you say...
>'Reebok, Because There's Nothing You Can't Do.'

Clive finishes. He is surprised to find Maurice in tears.
Clive is thrown totally off as Maurice stares at him angrily through streaming tears.

>MAURICE
>My wife is dead.

Maurice continues his powerful gaze until Clive looks away.
Clive gathers his things and leaves the chapel without

Walk of Remembrance- Trilogy Part 1

another word. Maurice drops his
head into his hands and
cries quietly.

CUT TO:

INT. HOSPITAL ROOM - NIGHT

A change of shifts. Stephanie
gathers her things. She lifts
her coat off the counter.
Underneath is a paper. She spins
the paper to face her. The
headline reads, "The End of a
Journey - Parker Hospitalized."

CUT TO:

HOSPITAL ROOM

Stephanie peeks into the dark room.

    STEPHANIE
  (whispers)
 Good night Mr. Parker.
I'll see
 you tomorrow.

Stephanie waits for a response from
the motionless figure on
the bed. She leaves the room a
little disappointed.

Walk of Remembrance- Trilogy Part 1

*WE MOVE CLOSER TO THE BED. We see Maurice laying still --
the battered photo of Ellen clutches to his chest.*

CUT TO:

INT. HOSPITAL HALL - DAY

Stephanie is wheeling Maurice down the hall. Maurice has a glint of happiness in his eye. They move through the doors marked "Visitor's Area."

Maurice stretches a huge grin as KRIS REDDY gets up from a chair. Kris bends down and hugs Maurice emotionally.

              KRIS
    Tom Joad?

             MAURICE
  ... The Grapes of Wrath.

              KRIS
    You're amazing.

CUT TO:

LATER

Walk of Remembrance- Trilogy Part 1

Maurice and Kris seated in the corner of the room.

                MAURICE
     I missed you Kris.

                KRIS
     I missed you to Mr. Parker.

                MAURICE
     Adelle told me, your writing is
     going well. The Crusader for
     social issues and all.

                KRIS
     You were right. From the heart is
     always better.

Beat.

                KRIS
     I drove by the bookstore -- it's
     boarded up now. There's a sign
     over the wood -- "Office space
     available."

The loss is evident on Maurice's eyes.

Walk of Remembrance- Trilogy Part 1

                    MAURICE
          I haven't been too punctual with
          the rent.

                    KRIS
          I was thinking you could open
          another store with investors. I'm
          sure a lot of people would want to
          get involved with you now.

Maurice forces a smile.

                    MAURICE
          Actually, I'm not worried about my
          career right now... I'm more
          worried about how you're getting me
          out of here?

Beat. Kris glances at the hair on his forearm.

                    MAURICE
          Are they standing?

                    KRIS
               (running his hand over his
                arm)

Walk of Remembrance- Trilogy Part 1

Saluting.

Beat.

                KRIS
Come on Mr. Parker.

               MAURICE
What, come on?

                KRIS
I can't do it. I want you to
finish, but I want you to live
more.

Maurice sits back straight. He looks upset.

               MAURICE
We do the operation after I finish.
I can't risk not finishing... I
thought you understood what I was
doing.

                KRIS
I do.

               MAURICE
Why in God's name did you fly all
the way here then?

Walk of Remembrance- Trilogy Part 1

                KRIS
       Don't do this.

              MAURICE
       ... To look me in the eye and say
       what's important to you isn't as
       important to me? To tell me you
       know what's best? To tell me life
       is more precious than what I feel
       for my wife?

Kris gets very emotional. He rises from this chair.

              KRIS
       Mr. Parker, you can yell at me, if
       it'll help. But I'm not risking
       your life.

              MAURICE
       It's mine to risk.

Maurice turns to the window away from Kris.

              KRIS
       Your operation is scheduled for

Walk of Remembrance- Trilogy Part 1

    Friday. I'll be back before then.

Kris walks to the door and stops.

      KRIS
    She knows you love her Mr. Parker.
    She knows now.

      MAURICE
    (not looking at Kris)
    No more words. Until I touch the
    ocean with my hands... it's all
    just words.

Kris is tortured. He leaves the room.

CUT TO:

INT. HOSPITAL HALL - DAY

Maurice wheels himself into the hall from the waiting area.
He looks around. His eyes lock on the EXIT SIGN over the
door at the end of the hall. His eyes scan the area quickly.
He immediately finds the guard on the floor staring at him.
The guard nods ever so slightly as if to say, "I know what

Walk of Remembrance- Trilogy Part 1

you're thinking." Maurice turns his attention to a small boy in a hospital gown, being scolded by a head nurse.

                  HEAD NURSE
      You cooperate with us about taking
      your medicine and maybe we'll talk
      about candy.

The head nurse takes a chocolate bar out of the boy's tiny hands. The boy offers no response. Maurice watches curiously as STEPHANIE walks over and pats the boys head. Maurice catches a small exchange -- Stephanie slips another candy bar into his pocket. The boy breaks into a warm smile. Stephanie puts her fingers against her lips and winks. Maurice takes this exchange in with great interest.

CUT TO:

INT. HOSPITAL ROOM - DAY

Stephanie steps into the room and prepares a tray of food. The SILHOUETTED FIGURE of Maurice seated near the bay window

Walk of Remembrance- Trilogy Part 1

turns to face her.

              STEPHANIE
    You should be in bed.

The face stares back from the shadows. She feels him watching.

              MAURICE
    What do your friends call you?

              STEPHANIE
    Steph.

              MAURICE
    Do you have a car, Steph?

Beat.

              STEPHANIE
    You should be in bed...

Stephanie moves to Maurice... She stops short when his face comes into view. His eyes are raw -- red. His face puffy.

              STEPHANIE
    You're in pain.

              MAURICE
    I need your help.

              STEPHANIE

Walk of Remembrance- Trilogy Part 1

>>They told me, you might try to talk
me into something... You need to
rest Mr. Parker... It's for your
own good.
>>(beat)
>>I've been following your story for
a long while. It's a beautiful
thing you did.

>>MAURICE
>>You ever lose somebody Stephanie?

>>STEPHANIE
>>Mr. Parker, I'm supposed to give
you your fish sticks.

Beat. Maurice melts her with his expression.

>>STEPHANIE
>>... My father.

>>MAURICE
>>Did you tell him everything you
wanted to? Did you do everything
you could while he was here?

Walk of Remembrance- Trilogy Part 1

She shakes her head "No" -- the tears welling up in her eyes.

              MAURICE
    If I don't do this Steph, my life
      isn't worth saving.

Maurice reaches out and squeezes her soft trembling hand.

              MAURICE
      Please, help me.

CUT TO:

INT. HOSPITAL HALLWAY - DAY

Stephanie throws a nervous smile to the guard as she escorts a doctor down the hall... The doctor's oversized while lab coat almost drags on the floor as he tries to hide the pain of being on his feet. MAURICE PARKER studies a bogus chart in his hands. His new glasses, sliding off his nose. Beads of sweat -- revealing his agony.

CUT TO:

ELEVATOR

Walk of Remembrance- Trilogy Part 1

Three people in the elevator; Stephanie, Dr. Maurice Parker, and a female physician. The female doctor looks at Maurice curiously, studying his demeanor -- she can't place him.

The ELEVATOR DOORS OPEN on the third floor... The SOUND OF A TV FLOODS THE ELEVATOR COMPARTMENT. Maurice looks up in horror to see a close-up of his FACE superimposed on the TV screen seated on the receptionist's desk. A man gets on the elevator.

The female doctor stares at the TV as the doors close -- she immediately turns to Maurice... her view is blocked by the new passenger... the elevator progresses down 2... 1... The female doctor leans forward trying to get a glimpse of Maurice... THE BELL DINGS as the doors open on the ground floor.

Doctor Maurice Parker and Stephanie quickly exit... the female doctor stays in the elevator and watches carefully.

                        FEMALE DOCTOR

Walk of Remembrance- Trilogy Part 1

                    (yells)
              Excuse me, doctor...

DOWN THE HALL... Maurice pauses and
turns around -- fear
etched across his face. The female
doctor looks around the
barren hall then turns back to
Maurice.

                         FEMALE DOCTOR
              Good luck.

The female doctor smiles as the
doors shut. After a few
moments of shock -- Maurice smiles
back.

Stephanie yanks Maurice down the
hall and out the EMERGENCY
ROOM EXIT.

CUT TO:

EXT. STREET - DAY

A colorful canopy of leaves... a
familiar torn American flag.
Stephanie's white VW Rabbit pulls
to a stop.

                         MAURICE
              This is it... This is
        where I fell.

Walk of Remembrance- Trilogy Part 1

He turns back to Stephanie who stares back at him emotionally.

                STEPHANIE
    I never thanked my father. He did
      so much for me... I never thanked
      him.

Maurice holds her sad face in his scared hands.

                MAURICE
      (whispering)
    It's not too late.

Maurice gets out of the car painfully slow. He pulls his shoulder back upright with a laborious breath. A sense of pride returns to his face. He turns back to Stephanie and catches a horrified look. He follows her stare...

She is staring at his shirt... He looks down to see a DARK CRIMSON STAIN GROWING beneath the surface. He covers the area with his hand.

                MAURICE
    You're going to have a lot of work

                    to do when I get back.

                              STEPHANIE
                    Someone should be with
you.

Beat.

                              MAURICE
                    Someone is.

He gives her his best smile and
begins shuffling his feet
over the loose gravel of the
road... one step at a time.

CUT TO:

INT. HOSPITAL STAIRS - AFTERNOON

A black man -- grey, balding hair
walks hurriedly up the
stairs. This is STAN NEWTON.

Keeping in step with Newton is a
police officer. SERGEANT
EMORY, jet white hair, army cut,
gives him an intimidating
appearance.

CUT TO:

OUTSIDE DOOR

Walk of Remembrance- Trilogy Part 1

Newton stops Emory before entering.

>   NEWTON
>   I'm afraid Mrs. Matlin is very
>   upset.

Emory lets the warning sink in before opening the door. Adelle's VOICE IS BOOMING.

CUT TO:

HOSPITAL ROOM

Adelle YELLS at Dr. Ray, a few nurses, and the guard who was on duty.

>   ADELLE
>   ... "American Journal of
>   Psychology", "Psychological
>   Review", and "Science", so I think
>   it's safe to say my opinion is
>   valid.

She catches her breath.

>   ADELLE
>   How does a grown man who can barely

Walk of Remembrance- Trilogy Part 1

>>>>>>>>>>>>>>>>walk, just stroll out?...
This is
>>>>>>>>>>>>>>>>not James Bond here, this is my
>>>>>>>>>>>>>>>>uncle who owns a bookstore, and
>>>>>>>>>>>>>>>>gets outwitted by grade school kids
>>>>>>>>>>>>>>>>pulling pranks!

Adelle notices the new people in the room.

>>>>>>>>>>>>>>>>>>>>>>>>NEWTON
>>>>>>>>>>>>>>>>Mrs. Matlin, this is Sergeant
>>>>>>>>>>>>>>>>Emory. He'll help us find your
>>>>>>>>>>>>>>>>uncle.

Adelle walks up to Emory.

>>>>>>>>>>>>>>>>>>>>>>>>ADELLE
>>>>>>>>>>>>>>>>Let me tell you a story Sergeant.
>>>>>>>>>>>>>>>>There was a patient of mine who had
>>>>>>>>>>>>>>>>a Golden Retriever, Mac... She
>>>>>>>>>>>>>>>>loved Mac, not like a pet, but like
>>>>>>>>>>>>>>>>a family member. One day, she had
>>>>>>>>>>>>>>>>to leave Mac with 'friends', and

Walk of Remembrance- Trilogy Part 1

              wouldn't you know it, Mac gets away
              and ends up falling into a sewer.
              My patient comes back -- goes nuts
              when she hears that Mac has been in
              the sewer for over 48 hours.
              Apparently the cop who found the
              dog didn't want to get his pants
              dirty. And neither did anyone
              else. So of course, my patient
              decides to go in after it... she
              falls... breaks her hip and lands
              next to her dead dog, who died of
              toxic fumes down there...

Adelle looks around at all the engrossed faces.

                      ADELLE
              The moral of the story is... She
              sued for a lot of money! She sued
              the friends, the city, and the

>   officer for negligence on
> duty.
>   She has no Mac, no
> happiness, but
>   she's very rich now...
> That was a
>   dog. We're talking about
> a human
>   being...
>   (beat)
>   I hope everyone clearly
> understands
>   the chain of events that
> will occur
>   if something should
> happen to my
>   uncle, whom I love more
> than you
>   can possibly imagine...
> Now
>   Sergeant I would like to
> know right
>   now, if you're willing to
> get your
>   pants dirty for my uncle?

Adelle and Emory have a staring contest. Adelle wins. Adelle stands alone in a room with four men, and she is clearly the one in charge.

The door flies open. A police officer walks in pushing KRIS REDDY through the door.

Walk of Remembrance- Trilogy Part 1

                    OFFICER
          I found him sneaking up
the back
          stairs with this.

The officer holds out a long coat
and hat. Emory walks up to
Kris.

                    EMORY
          Did you help Mr. Parker
leave this
          hospital?

Kris looks to the empty bed and
smiles... a BIG SMILE.

                    KRIS
          No... But I was going to.

Beat. Emory turns to the officer
and ushers him to the door.

                    EMORY
          Forget him. It's time to
get our
          pants dirty.

Adelle smiles.

                    EMORY
          I want three black and
whites from
          here to Handley Avenue.
And no

Walk of Remembrance- Trilogy Part 1

                    communication with the
station.
                    The press monitors the
                    transmissions.

                         KRIS
                    (a born actor)
                    They can do that?

                         EMORY
                    That goes for all of you.
Not a
                    word about this
disappearance to
                    anyone. Absolutely no
press.

Kris smiles innocently.

CUT TO:

EXT. STREET - NIGHT

Police vehicles roam the city
streets -- slowing to a crawl
at every white male over forty,
walking the sidewalks.

CUT TO:

ADELLE

scanning the crowded intersections
through the open window of

Walk of Remembrance- Trilogy Part 1

her moving taxi.

CUT TO:

KRIS

patrolling the streets on foot. He stops at a hot dog vendor and flashes a picture of Maurice from his wallet. The vendor shakes his head, "No."

A COMMOTION BREAKS OUT ONE BLOCK DOWN... Kris spins in that direction... sees a crowd forming at the corner of the sidewalk... Starts toward them... Kris sees something through the thinner parts of the crowd... something laying on the sidewalk... A man! Kris' walk turns into a sprint.

Kris works his way through the growing crowd, puncturing the center of the circle... Kris gazes down at the man writhing on the concrete... A black man, shaking uncontrollably. A women standing over the fallen man waves the crowd back.

            WOMAN
    He has Epilepsy, just give him

Walk of Remembrance- Trilogy Part 1

room... An ambulance is on the way.

The crowd spreads out. Kris looks down at the unconscious
man on the sidewalk sadly -- Kris' thoughts race. He moves
on with newfound concern.

CUT TO:

INT. HOMELESS SHELTER - EVENING

A converted gymnasium. The room is splintered into rows of
folding tables and chairs. Against the wall, is the serving
stand. Groups of volunteers dispense sandwiches and soup.

IN THE CORNER

The room is crowded with homeless men and women and a few
children. In the back we find MAURICE. In his old clothes,
and tired disheveled appearance -- Maurice is virtually
invisible in this crowd. He presses something to his injured
side. His condition has worsened.

He eyes the entrance where a POLICE OFFICER walks in and

Walk of Remembrance- Trilogy Part 1

moves to the serving counter. The officer asks the serving lady something, and shows her a picture. She shrugs her shoulders and continues serving. The cop takes one last look around the hundreds of hungry people leaving the room.

Maurice pulls up his hand from underneath his shirt. The napkin he was holding at his side is SATURATED WITH BLOOD. Maurice replaces it with a clean napkin.

DISSOLVE TO:

EXT. POLICE STATION - MORNING

SUNRISE ON SOUTHERN CALIFORNIA.

CUT TO:

INT. POLICE STATION - MORNING

Emory rubs his eyes as the papers pile up on his desk. OFFICER KLEIN lays out the newspapers one after the other.

              KLEIN
    ... L.A. Times -- 'He's Back.'...

Walk of Remembrance- Trilogy Part 1

   San Francisco Chronicle -- 'Have
   You Seen Maurice?'... New York Post
   'Unstoppable!'

Klein lays the last paper on the table.

      EMORY
  Is that all?

      KLEIN
  No. The Mayor sent word, that he
  wants this thing handled quickly,
  before anything unfortunate
  happens. He said he doesn't want
  to be known as the 'Mayor of the
  City Where Maurice Parker Died!'

      EMORY
  Is that all?

      KLEIN
  No. Mrs. Matlin's waiting for
  you.

Klein opens the door. Adelle walks in and stands at a

distance from Emory. She looks beat. Her eyes are bloodshot, and tired.

> ADELLE
> What happened with the museum
> sighting?

> EMORY
> False alarm.

Adelle is visibly dejected.

> EMORY
> It's been a long couple of days for
> all of us. So let me be honest.
> If he hasn't turned up yet, he's
> probably --

> ADELLE
> No... No.

> EMORY
> I spoke with Dr. Ray this morning,
> and he said it was highly unlikely
> that someone in his condition could
> survive this long without medical

Walk of Remembrance- Trilogy Part 1

           attention, let alone walk sixty
           miles -- in fact his exact word
           was, 'Impossible'.

Adelle fiddles with her coat.

               EMORY
           If I knew where he was, I'd get him
           off the street, but I think it's
           time that you, the Mayor, and
           everyone else be braced for the
           inevitable.

CUT TO:

EXT. JUNIPERO SERRA FREEWAY - DAY

The freeway is packed -- bumper to bumper. Cars standing still in the hot sun.

A hispanic man in his late forties, JUAN is seated in his Dodge Caravan when he sees someone in his rearview mirror. A man is using a stick as a cane. The struggling man makes his way along the shoulder very slowly.

Walk of Remembrance- Trilogy Part 1

Juan reaches over to his passenger seat and turns over the L.A. Times. Under the heading, "He's Back!" is Maurice's picture. Juan quickly rolls down his window as Maurice passes by on the shoulder.

> JUAN
> (yelling)
> Hey, Maurice man -- keep going
> buddy!

Maurice is startled at the man's yell, but then smiles when the words register. Maurice struggles forward.

Juan keeps yelling encouragements... This grabs the attention of other drivers who realize who is walking past them. One by one, car doors open and people call to Maurice.

> OVERWEIGHT WOMAN
> Don't stop Maurice!

> YOUNG MAN
> Go Mr. Parker!

Cars start to HONK... More and more people turn to see the

Walk of Remembrance- Trilogy Part 1

commotion... The YELLING AND
HONKING IS JOINED BY WHISTLES
AND CHEERS --

Maurice can't believe it -- he
tries to smile but can't hold
it. His face tightens with every
step. His shirt is soiled
with blood. He raises his hand and
gives a weak wave to a
woman who holds up her little boy
through the sunroof of the
car.

CUT TO:

A WCAU NEWS VAN

parked in the traffic. A
NEWSREPORTER stares through
binoculars.

                    REPORTER
        Thank you God!

The crew quickly prepares their
cameras and equipment. They
move like lightning. In seconds
they are shooting the crowd
and their hero.

The air is CHARGED... THE NOISE
GROWING, MORE AND MORE PEOPLE
JOIN IN... LOUDER... People stand
on top of their cars to get

Walk of Remembrance- Trilogy Part 1

a better view...

CUT TO:

A POLICE CAR

stuck in traffic. OFFICER DAWSON looks around as the PARADE OF NOISE SURGES TOWARDS HIM. He looks out his window and catches a GLIMPSE OF MAURICE LIMPING UP THE FREEWAY.

     DAWSON
 Sweet Jesus!

CUT TO:

INT. POLICE STATION - DAY

Officer Klein busts into Emory's office just as Adelle is about to leave.

     KLEIN
 They found him.

Adelle is instantly charged with life.

     KLEIN
 Dawson's on the C.B. -- wants to
  talk with you Sarg.

Walk of Remembrance- Trilogy Part 1

CUT TO:

RADIO ROOM

Adelle and as many officers that will fit in the room are listening to the radio conversation.

                EMORY
    What's going on? Where is he?

Emory CLICKS TO LISTEN. THE SPEAKERS EXPLODE WITH HONKING AND CHEERING -- IT SOUNDS LIKE A CARNIVAL. DAWSON YELLS OVER THE COMMOTION.

                DAWSON (V.O.)
    He's just getting off 280. It's
    amazing Sarg... everybody's out of
    their cars and cheering him on.

                EMORY
    Shit, get him in your car and take
    him to St. Vincents.

Beat.

Walk of Remembrance- Trilogy Part 1

                    DAWSON (V.O.)
          You ever see that concert footage
          of the Doors, Sarg?

Adelle and the room of officers look confused.

                    EMORY
          What the hell are you talking
          about?

                    DAWSON (V.O.)
          The Doors, the musical group. I
          saw a documentary where the police
          stopped one of their concerts,
          snatched Jim Morrison right off the
          stage... the crowd went frickin
          nuts -- they tore up the place --
          it turned into a war.
              (beat)
          ... I'm not stopping this concert
          by myself. And there's no way
          you're getting backup here -- it's
          jammed up for miles.

Emory is thinking fast.

> DAWSON (V.O.)
> Why don't we just let him finish Sarg?

Beat. Emory looks at Adelle's expectant face. He talks into the C.B. without taking his eyes off her.

> EMORY
> How does he look?

> DAWSON (V.O.)
> Like shit. He's bleeding heavily. He's having breathing problems and he's as pale as stone. If he wasn't moving, I'd swear he was dead.

Emory thinks. He talks to the other officers in the room.

> EMORY
> Bring him in. Now! If he dies out there, who the hell knows what that crowd will do...
> (to himself)

Walk of Remembrance- Trilogy Part 1

> Let alone the Mayor.

The room empties fast. Emory talks to Adelle.

> EMORY
> He'll be in a hospital within a
> half an hour.

Somehow, Adelle's face doesn't convey much confidence.

CUT TO:

INT. PACIFICA MALL - DAY

The shops are empty. The food court abandoned.

Close to five hundred people are huddled at the center of the mall. The HI-FI HOUSE has four large screen TV's in their bay windows and speakers on the outside of the doors to lure passing shoppers in.

All four sets have the same program on -- A NEWSBREAK on Maurice Parker. The crowd listening anxiously.

> TV ANCHOR

Walk of Remembrance- Trilogy Part 1

>   ... He's headed West on
> Sharp Park
>   Road... Witnesses
> describe him as
>   seriously injured.

A shock of concern shoots through the crowd.

>   TV ANCHOR
>   Lynn McCay and our
> Highway Cam --
>   has just spotted him...

The picture cuts to a HELICOPTER SHOT OF DOWNTOWN PACIFICA -- at first it just looks like an aerial of buildings, then the camera ZOOMS. It catches a tiny figure struggling through a street intersection.

CUT TO:

EXT. STREET - DAY

Newspapers spiral through the air. Maurice stretches his neck up, squinting at the sun. The SILHOUETTE OF A HELICOPTER hovers above him. The NOISE is overpowering.

Maurice's fatigue grows, every muscle, every ounce of energy

Walk of Remembrance- Trilogy Part 1

goes into each step. Maurice clutches the side of his head... the steps halted... hands trembling, teeth clenched, eyes squeezed shut. A surge of intense pain tries to buckle him... Maurice fights it off as he moves his feet again.

The helicopter SWOOPS above as he makes his turn onto a FINAL STRETCH OF ROAD adjacent to the BEACH.

Maurice stops dead in his tracks as he turns the corner to find a SEA OF PEOPLE WAITING FOR HIM. A momentous sight... people lined along the street for as far as the eye can see. AN EXPLOSION OF YELLING, CHEERING CALIFORNIAN'S ENGULFS THE AIR as they spot Maurice standing at the end of the street. The CROWD SURGES TOWARDS HIM.

Maurice is dazed... the noise, the pain, the faces swirl in his head as thousands of people surround him. Maurice is overwhelmed. He is about to collapse when someone takes hold of his arm. Maurice turns to see KRIS REDDY STANDING NEXT TO HIM. In the midst of this chaos and growing madness.

Walk of Remembrance- Trilogy Part 1

Maurice and Kris have an entire conversation with one emotional look.

The SOUNDS of SIRENS BREAK the moment. Kris turns to see two police cars turn on the street behind them.

Kris turns to Maurice.

      KRIS
  Don't stop walking.

Kris lets go of his arm and moves like lightning. He jumps atop a fire-hydrant and yells to the crowd.

      KRIS
  The police are here. They're
  coming to take Mr. Parker away. He
  needs our help.

Kris points to the squad cars inching their way up the street.

      KRIS
  Help Mr. Parker! Don't let them
  end the walk.

Walk of Remembrance- Trilogy Part 1

CUT TO:

THE SQUAD CARS

AS THEY COME TO A HALT as a wall of people stand in their way. The SPEAKER ON THE POLICE CAR BLARES THROUGH THE AIR.

                    SPEAKER
    Step aside now! You are ordered to
    step aside now!

The people don't move. A WOMAN carrying a BABY makes the baby move her little hand in a waving gesture to the officers behind the wheel of the police cars. The officers look at each other in disbelief.

CUT TO:

EXT. STREET - DAY

The far end of the beach road. A POLICE CAR SCREECHES TO A STOP. Sergeant Emory and Adelle get out.

Adelle is completely blown away. She looks around at the

Walk of Remembrance- Trilogy Part 1

PANDEMONIUM. Thousands of men, women and children
celebrating with APPLAUSE AND CHEERS, HELICOPTERS IN THE AIR, camera crews standing on raised platforms. Adelle drinks in the ELECTRIC ATMOSPHERE with awe.

Emory yells orders into his WALKIE-TALKIE as Adelle breaks the outer edge of the crowd and disappears into the field of spectators.

              EMORY
        (yelling)
   What the hell is going on? It's frickin wall to wall people and they're way too emotional. We need mucho backup -- now!... Officers are to bring in Mr. Parker on sight, don't ask questions, don't hesitate, bring him in... I want a barricade placed along the entire beach area... Now God damn it, now!

Walk of Remembrance- Trilogy Part 1

Emory CLICKS OFF and looks around at the growing crowd -- he turns to see a PUBLIC BUS UNLOADING PASSENGERS -- fifty more spectators rush off the bus and rush toward the crowded street.

                    EMORY
      Holy shit.

CUT TO:

EXT. STREET - DAY

Maurice stares down at the ground... willing each new step. THE CHEERS AND WORDS OF ENCOURAGEMENT BLURRING INTO A UNDISTINGUISHABLE SOUND.

Maurice looks up for a moment as something grabs his attention -- Maurice gasps for air as his eyes focus... The small faces become clearer... Maurice stands twenty feet from the entire population of PACIFICA HIGH SCHOOL. They cover one side of the street for an entire block. Stretched over their heads, held up by twenty students is a HUGE HAND PAINTED BANNER. Maurice reads the words:

Walk of Remembrance- Trilogy Part 1

                    "ELLEN IS
WATCHING!"

CUT TO:

EXT. BEACH - DAY

Trucks unload dozens upon dozens of
blue-wooden barricades.
An assembly line of officers place
the barricades end to end
at the place where the sand meets
the pavement.

Emory yells orders as a new truck
arrives.

CUT TO:

INT. NEWS MONTAGE - DAY

SHOTS OF THE PULSATING CROWD...
GLIMPSES OF MAURICE MOVING
THROUGH THE CENTER OF THIS MASS.
OVER THESE PICTURES WE HEAR
SNIPPETS OF VOICES OF TV ANCHOR
PEOPLE, RADIO PERSONALITIES
AND ANNOUNCERS ALL OVER THE
COUNTRY, DISSOLVING INTO EACH
OTHER ONE AFTER THE OTHER...

                    TV ANCHOR
(V.O.)

Walk of Remembrance- Trilogy Part 1

>   ... Through ten states and over
>   three thousand miles...

                    TV ANCHOR 2 (V.O.)
>   ... A bookstore owner from
>   Philadelphia Pennsylvania...

CUT TO:

FATHER BERCHMAN

the father that brought Maurice in out of the cold in the Midwest, praying intensely in his chapel. AN OLD HAND-HELD RADIO IS ON THE PEW NEXT TO HIM. He listens to the updates.

                    RADIO D.J. (V.O.)
>   ... Ellen Parker killed by a drunk
>   driver September 2nd...

CUT TO:

MR. CALDWELL

Isaac's father, sitting in a TV station watching the monitors

Walk of Remembrance - Trilogy Part 1

as the feeds come in from
California. Mr. Caldwell watches
with great emotion, eyes glued to
the screen.

                      TV ANCHOR 3
(V.O.)
        ... A seven month odyssey
through
        the heart of the
country...

CUT TO:

SERGEANT DALLY

the police officer from
Philadelphia who worked with
Adelle.
He listens with the rest of the
precinct to a portable stereo
on a windowsill. The room is
silent -- everyone hangs on the
words coming from the speakers.

                      RADIO D.J. 2
(V.O.)
        ... the power of the
human
        spirit...

CUT TO:

GERALD

Walk of Remembrance- Trilogy Part 1

in a hotel room. The TV FILLING THE ROOM WITH NEWS. Gerald sits behind two large room-service carts of food. He takes a big bite of a sandwich with an emotional smile to the television.

                    TV ANCHOR 4 (V.O.)
    ... A life threatening condition,
        Transient Cerebral Ischemia...

CUT TO:

ST. VINCENT'S HOSPITAL

where STEPHANIE watches in the jam packed recreation room with about thirty patients watching a TV screen mounted high in the corner of the room. Stephanie looks a mess, she's been crying for a while.

                    TV ANCHOR 5
    ... a journey he began by himself,
    will end with a family of millions
    at his side...

Walk of Remembrance- Trilogy Part 1

CUT TO:

EXT. STREET - DAY

The BOISTEROUS crowd parts like a ripple effect as Maurice walks through. The eyes fall emotionally on him as he stares down at the ground trying to keep moving.

Maurice gasps harder now, his eyes stinging with drops of sweat falling from his brow. People in the crowd cover their mouths in shock as they get a clear view of him... His shirt soaked on one side with blood, his entire body shaking with pain, and exhaustion, his face hollow and pale -- ghostly.

Maurice stops in his tracks. He looks up at a wooden sign, worn from the years of salt water air. The sign reads:

        "PACIFICA BEACH - 1/2 MILE"

Maurice's thoughts fade away from this place, this time...

CUT TO:

Walk of Remembrance- Trilogy Part 1

EXT. PHILADELPHIA - FIFTEEN YEARS AGO - NIGHT (FLASHBACK)

WE ARE IN THE PARKER BEDROOM. The lights are off. The
MOONLIGHT FROM THE WINDOWS BLANKETS Young Maurice and Young
Ellen as they lay in bed. Ellen is cradled in Maurice's
arms. She is awake and watching the shadows dance on the
ceiling. She speaks in whispers.

          ELLEN
  What do you think heaven is like?

Maurice opens his eyes and stares at his beautiful wife.

          MAURICE
  I don't know.

          ELLEN
  I think it's a different place for
  each person.

          MAURICE
  Did you have a dream?

Beat.

          ELLEN

Walk of Remembrance- Trilogy Part 1

        I know where my heaven is.

              MAURICE
        Where?

              ELLEN
        Pacifica, California.

Maurice chuckles.

              MAURICE
        Why there?

              ELLEN
        When I was ten, my family lived in
        Pacifica for a year. I used to go
        to the beach everyday that summer.
        I never felt so happy, carefree.
        It was a magic place for me...
        That's where my heaven will be.

Beat.

              ELLEN
        Maurice?

              MAURICE
        Yes.

Walk of Remembrance- Trilogy Part 1

                    ELLEN
        If I die, you'll know where to look
            for me?

                  MAURICE
        Go to sleep Ellen.

                  ELLEN
        No really, if God takes us away
            from each other, you know where to
            look now?

Beat.

                  MAURICE
            (pacifying her)
        The beach of Pacifica, California.

                  ELLEN
        Good.

Beat.

                  MAURICE
        Go to sleep Ellen.

Ellen smiles as she cradles deeper into Maurice's arms.
Husband and wife fall asleep together.

Walk of Remembrance- Trilogy Part 1

CUT TO:

EXT. PACIFICA BEACH SIGN - DAY (PRESENT)

Maurice snaps back to the present, the PAIN AND COMMOTION come back in a tidal wave of reality.

Maurice wipes the tears in his eyes and tries to take a step. Someone blocks his way.

                ADELLE
    Uncle Maurice, please, we have to
      get you to a hospital.

Adelle looks at her wounded Uncle sadly. She touches his shirt and her hand comes away with blood.

                MAURICE
      I have to finish first.

                ADELLE
      I won't let you die.

The inner circle of people bursts open, as KRIS BREAKS THROUGH.

                KRIS

Walk of Remembrance- Trilogy Part 1

>>>>>>>>>>Let him finish Adelle.
He's almost
>>>>>>>>>>there.

>>>>>>>>>>>>>>>>ADELLE
>>>>>>>>>>>>>>(yelling)
>>>>>>>>>>He's almost dead. Can't you see
>>>>>>>>>>that! This has nothing to do with
>>>>>>>>>>you.

Maurice touches Adelle's cheek turning her attention back to him. He barely manages to get the words out.

>>>>>>>>>>>>>>>>MAURICE
>>>>>>>>>>It has nothing to do with you
>>>>>>>>>>either... This is between Ellen and
>>>>>>>>>>me.

Beat. Maurice begins crying uncontrollably.

>>>>>>>>>>>>>>>>MAURICE
>>>>>>>>>>I'm begging you...

Maurice takes her hand and bends down putting his forehead to her hand as if getting blessings from her.

>>>>>>>>>>>>>>>>MAURICE

Walk of Remembrance- Trilogy Part 1

             Let me do this for Ellen,
let me do
          this for my wife.

Adelle's heart is breaking. She
weeps openly as she
straightens her Uncle to an upright
position. She wipes the
tears from his eyes with her hand
gently.

AT THAT MOMENT THE INNER CIRCLE
BREAKS OPEN AS TWO OFFICERS
RUSH IN. They reach for Maurice.

                    ADELLE
          Touch him, and they'll be
a riot...

Adelle stands firm, the strength in
her growing with each
second.

                    ADELLE
          ... and I'll start it.

The officers are taken off guard.
They look around at the
countless sea of eyes on them.
Adelle sees they won't do
anything and moves to Maurice's
side.

Maurice begins to walk again.
Adelle to one side, Kris to

Walk of Remembrance- Trilogy Part 1

the other and thousands of people
following in step.

CUT TO:

EXT. BEACH FRONT - DAY

The wave of people led by Maurice
walk toward the beach. The
beach is blocked off by barricades
all along it's perimeter.
Police officers stand every ten
feet along it's edge.

A young officer watches fearfully
as the ocean of people move
towards him. OFFICER GANTZ TALKS
INTO HIS WALKIE-TALKIE.

                    GANTZ
          He's coming. What should
I do?

CUT TO:

SERGEANT EMORY

at the other end of the beach
barricade, holding back
hundreds of people trying to get to
the beach. Emory holds
his walkie-talkie and looks around
at the sea of anxious

Walk of Remembrance- Trilogy Part 1

faces. He makes eye contact with a woman in tears.

CUT TO:

OFFICER GANTZ

clicking off his walkie-talkie as the crowd presses up to the barricade. Officer Gantz is in awe as Maurice appears from the crowd -- looking like a ghost of war... a holy apparition. Maurice works his way painfully to Gantz.

Gantz looks into Maurice's pleading eyes. Maurice tries to say something, but nothing can come out...

Gantz turns away from Maurice and picks up one of the barricades. He makes an opening about three feet wide. Gantz turns back to Maurice, stands at attention, and steps aside.

                    GANTZ
             (with unspeakable
               admiration)
          Watch your step Mr. Parker.

Walk of Remembrance- Trilogy Part 1

Adelle and Kris watch in amazement as Maurice TAKES HIS FIRST STEP ONTO THE SAND.

CUT TO:

EXT. BEACH - DAY

An empty beach. ALL SOUND AND CHAOS DISAPPEARS. THE GENTLE HISS OF THE OCEAN FILLS THE AIR.

The last fifty yards...

The steps in the sand, heavy, torturous. Each step, a step closer to her...

Maurice picks up the pace. His numb feet making prints in the sand. His lungs on fire...

Twenty feet left... Ten... Five...

The COOL WATER engulfs his feet and ankles. Maurice falls to his knees like a man falling before God.

Kneeling in the water, Maurice raises his hands to his eyes. The water spills between his fingers... clear, pure, magical.

Walk of Remembrance- Trilogy Part 1

*Maurice GASPS hard as he falls onto his back. The water
comes in and washes over him...
Gasping harder... He's
staring into the sky... Another
wave of ocean gently blankets
him... Gasp... He spots something
above him, fluttering...
his vision BLURS... WHITE
FLUTTERING... SLOW-MOTION. THE
IMAGE CLEARS... Maurice smiles as
he makes out the image of a
WHITE DOVE FLYING ABOVE HIM...*

*Maurice takes a short breath, very
short. His body goes
still -- his eyes stay fixes at one
point... No more pain, no
more loss, no more words...*

*The water washes over Maurice A.
Parker...
Over his lifeless body...
And over his smile...*

FADE TO BLACK.

Printed in Great Britain
by Amazon